And Justice For All

And Justice For All

THE LEGAL RIGHTS
OF YOUNG PEOPLE

by Sandra Joseph Nunez

and

Trish Marx

The Millbrook Press
Brookfield, Connecticut

Photographs courtesy of NCLC: p. 19; Patricia Stevens/YWCA of Brooklyn: p. 25; The George Sim Johnston Archives of The New York Society for the Prevention of Cruelty to Children: p. 28; AP/Wide World: pp. 39, 83, 104; Bettmann: pp. 56, 109,140; Impact Visuals: pp. 65 (© Richard Renaldi), 90 (© Kirk Condyles), 132 (© Jim Tynan); Culver Pictures: p. 115.

Published by The Millbrook Press, Inc.
2 Old New Milford Road, Brookfield, Connecticut 06804

Library of Congress Cataloging-in-Publication Data
Nunez, Sandra Joseph.
And justice for all: the legal rights of young people / by Sandra Joseph Nunez and Trish Marx.
p.   cm.
Summary: Examines various legal issues, including free speech, privacy, child labor, and discrimination, as they apply to minors.
Includes bibliographical references and index.
ISBN 0-7613-0068-6 (lib. bdg.)
1. Children—Legal status, laws, etc.—United States—Juvenile literature.
2. Children's rights—United States—Juvenile literature.
[1. Children's rights. 2. Law.] I. Marx, Trish. II. Title. III. Series.
KF479.Z9N86   1997   346.7301'35—dc21   96-40523   CIP   AC

Contents

For my children, Manelle, Justin, and Alexander
SJN

To my parents, with love and thanks
TM

Thank you to my first "Legal Beagles" class at the Englewood Cliffs Public School, whose enthusiasm inspired this project. I am indebted to Martin Guggenheim and Mark Mattaini for contributing their precious time and professional expertise to work with me to strengthen this book. My appreciation to Mary Opulente Krener who found a resolution for every problem, Diane Christian, Charmaine Jefferson, Emily Kambour, Barbara Lucas, the staff of the Englewood Library, Amy Shields who showed me what editing is all about, and finally my family who makes everything possible—my parents, Victor and Dorothy Joseph, and my husband Domingo, for their constant support, and my children for their invaluable perspective.

Sandra Joseph Nunez

The boys from Collegiate School in New York City, class of 1995, were immensely helpful in both eating pizza and in lending their thoughts to the book. Thank you, and thank you to Phyllis Brugnolotti, the Collegiate School librarian for her endless sharing of resources and time. Kristin McDonough opened the vast resources of Baruch College Library to us; my children were, as usual, my first line of defense (*How can you write a book about rights when we have none!!*); Anne Morris shared her thoughts and experience; Barbara Lucas was an unfailing source of encouragement for years; and I learned Sandra was not only brilliant in life, but in law as well.

Trish Marx

And Justice For All

Introduction

The term "children's rights" is generally applied to all the protections and privileges needed for a safe and healthy childhood. The legal definition is much narrower. A child's legal rights include only those laws—constitutional laws, federal and state laws, and common laws (court decisions)— that give minors specific rights and protections enforceable in a court of law. These include the right to an education, the right to inherit property, and the right to a fair trial.

According to law, a minor is any person who has not reached the age of majority, as specified by state law. (This book uses the terms minor, child, and youth interchangeably.) Since the voting age was lowered to eighteen in 1971, most states mark this as the age of majority, when a child is released from the control of his or her parents to assume most of the rights and responsibilities of an adult.

As is true of most areas of the law, rules contract and expand according to the needs and demands of the times. This book presents a picture of the minor as recognized by law, looking at case histories and events that forced both the courts and the legislatures to reexamine the legal status of the child in American society. Integral to this theme is the changing role of the parent and state (the government) in making decisions for the child. Although it will not replace statute books or the advice of an attorney, this book will give children and adults a broader understanding of laws that involve minors.

Foreword

This important book explores the gradual recognition of young people's rights to a voice in legal matters that affect them and gives readers a clear vision of why that matters. History teaches us that the interests of those who have weak voices in directing their lives, whether they be women, people of color, or youth, are often poorly protected. Oppression and exploitation are often the results.

In this book, the authors clarify each of the major legal issues that affects children and young people, from child custody to criminal issues, from freedom of speech to discrimination. In each case, they begin with high-visibility cases that draw attention to central issues. They then discuss the history of each issue and outline the current status and unanswered questions. The material is handled in a way that will be of value not only to child advocates and other adults but also to young people themselves, perhaps the most crucial audience for this volume.

Young people who know their legal rights may be able to protect themselves in potentially dangerous situations. For example, many probably do not know that they can call 911 if they feel they are in danger of physical abuse. How many lives might have been protected and preserved if this were common knowledge? Secondly, knowing that they have a place in deliberations that affect them may lead young people to view the legal system and, by extension, society as legitimate protections rather than instruments of oppression and coercion. As a result, they may come to recognize and respect their own places in society.

Legal situations in which some participants have weak voices, in the form of limited rights, inevitably result in the use of adversarial and coercive power. When young people have a knowledge of their rights an important shift results. It is far more likely that constructive solutions that work for everyone will emerge when all parties recognize the validity of each other's differing forms of power and the validity of each other's voices. Knowing and exercising their legal rights is an important dimension of this process for young people, and will also often contribute to the quality of their lives, their safety, and sometimes their very survival. This book is a step toward protection and success for our children.

Mark A. Mattaini, DSW, CSW
Associate Professor
Columbia University
School of Social Work

CHAPTER ONE

A THREE-PRONGED SYSTEM OF JUSTICE

Let us speak less of the duties of children and more of their rights.

Jean Jacques Rousseau (1712–1778)

From British colonial times in the 1600s until the late nineteenth century, the concept of children's rights was virtually nonexistent. In the eyes of the law, children were viewed as possessions of their parents. Parents had the exclusive authority to decide how to raise their children. The state observed a hands-off policy, believing that the interests of the parents and children were one and the same and that "the obligation of parental duty is so well secured by the strength of natural affection, it seldom requires to be enforced by human laws."[1] This arrangement worked because, in most cases, the underlying assumption that parents protected their children's welfare was true. But when it did not work, there was no established legal or social mechanism to protect the child. Children were sold, traded, or forced to work long hours under terrible conditions in order to supplement the family income with a few pennies a week. Children with no homes or family were indentured, or legally assigned, to people who would take them in and make them work as servants, farmhands, or apprentices with no pay.

A Massachusetts law of 1836 mandated that children would have at least three months of education during the year. But that was not strictly enforced, and it would take another century to see the earliest child-labor and compulsory-education laws in practice on a national scale. In the early nineteenth century, more than two million children, sixteen or younger, were working outside the home, often six days a week for twelve hours a day. Children as young as three or four picked cotton and peeled shrimp. Boys not much older barely saw the sun as they spent their days underground in coal mines, and both girls and boys worked in cotton factories, breathing in lint and dust all day long. Strict discipline was enforced in and out of the home to prevent delinquency, disobedience, and laziness. Corporal punishment was a way of life. Massachusetts law in 1854 recommended the death penalty for children above the age of sixteen who cursed or hit their mothers. This concept was not exclusive to this culture or this era. In England, historical records show that Lady Jane Grey, King Henry VI, John Wesley, and Samuel Pepys either were whipped as children or did not spare the rod on their own. Sir Thomas More, an enlightened man in all respects, beat his daughters with a peacock feather.

This 1909 photograph shows a young girl during one of her endless days at work in a textile mill, a dirty and potentially dangerous workplace that employed many children.

As America entered the twentieth century, the state began to use its "supreme power of guardianship," or *parens patiae*, and passed legislation to prevent the exploitation and abuse of children at home and in the workplace. Now there were parents on one side, and the state, which could make decisions in the best interest of the child, on the other. While the parents still retained the general right to determine how to raise their children, the state could limit parental control if the child needed protection (such as from severe physical abuse), or if the child had committed a crime, or when an overriding state interest (such as education for children) had to be safeguarded. Since the 1960s, this delicate balance of power between parents and the state has been disturbed by yet another entity claiming the right to protect its independent interests—the child. In instances where a child's interest or legal concern is legitimately different from the interest of the parent or the state, the child needs a legal right, enforceable in a court of law, to have the claim addressed.

The first step in this direction was taken in 1967 when the Supreme Court of the United States ruled that fifteen-year-old Gerald Gault was entitled to constitutional protections in juvenile court. (See Chapter 8.) Until then the Constitution applied only to adults. Justice Abe Fortas, in the majority decision, clearly defined a child's legal role by declaring: "We are to treat the child as an individual human being and not revert in spite of good intentions to the more primitive days when he was treated as chattel."[2] These words by Judge Fortas established that children were people too, and that they were entitled to constitutional protection. Later cases established a child's right to protest against public policies such as saluting the flag or demonstrating against the Vietnam War. Although children still needed help from their parents, and from attorneys, to apply these rights, they at last had them. And this raised a whole new set of issues.

The question facing courts now is whose rights are supreme? The tradition of parents in charge is still the general rule, but in certain circumstances courts have to decide if there need to be some exceptions to this rule. If there are compelling social reasons, does the state have the right to tell parents how to raise their children? Are the rights of parents to guide and mold their children being violated when the state dictates the terms? Are children being shortchanged by being denied freedoms and choices given only to adults?

Curfew laws are a good example of how conflicting interests come into play when a law seeks to restrict activities that are usually controlled by a parent. Some states, including New Jersey, California, and Florida, believe that crime will decrease and children will be safer if they are not allowed on the streets after a certain hour, usually 10:00 P.M. Parents who challenge these laws say they have the right to determine when their children should be off the streets. Teenagers protest the curfew laws on the grounds that they too have the constitutional right under the First Amendment to freedom of assembly (gathering in public). They also claim that they are being singled out and judged guilty before they commit a crime. In response, the courts have already ruled that the child's right to freedom of movement is secondary to the state's interest in protecting the child, and in maintaining a peaceful society. The parents' challenge to the courts has yet to be addressed.

Due to the long tradition in this country of the sacredness of the family, the courts are reluctant to interfere with parents in the raising of their children. The state has to prove it has a more important interest in order to supersede a parent's belief. In *Wisconsin* v. *Yoder* (1972), the Supreme Court ruled that the state could not force Amish parents to send their children to public high school if it violated Amish religious beliefs and customs. In other words, a state's interest in ensuring a high school education for a child was secondary to the religious traditions of the Amish parents. Only Justice William O. Douglas, in his dissenting decision, took the child into account when he wrote that every Amish child who was to be deprived of a high school education should have had the opportunity to testify independently about his or her religious beliefs before being deprived of this right. "On this important and vital matter of education, I think the children should be entitled to be heard....it is the student's judgment, not his parents, that is essential if we are to give full meaning to what we have said about the Bill of Rights and of the rights of students to be masters of their own destiny."[3]

A Florida court did something unprecedented in 1992 when the judge allowed the voice of twelve-year-old Gregory Kingsley to be heard and considered in a custody hearing to determine where and with whom he would live. Instead of relying only on Gregory's mother's assertions and recommendations by state child-care officials to resolve the issue, the judge also listened to Gregory and his lawyer. The case was exceptional in that a child protected his own interests, which differed from those of his parents, by taking an active role in a legal proceeding deciding his welfare.

Several other laws pertaining to truancy, welfare, sex education, abortion, and search and seizure are coming under this three-pronged scrutiny of the parent, the state, and the child. From the basic issues of shelter and support, to the more esoteric questions of the freedom to express opinions, the struggle for autonomy among parent, child, and state persists. Life at home, in school, in public, and on the job gives rise to the question of who will have the final word. Parents fiercely guard their traditional right to determine the ideal environment for their child. The state believes it has a responsibility to safeguard all members of society, especially the child. And the child, who is now being punished as an adult when found guilty of an adult crime, is demanding to be treated more like an adult in other areas of life.

With such conflicting convictions, the struggle is surfacing more frequently and becoming more heated. This book will examine and explain the issues as they have evolved in and out of court. And perhaps—when the inevitable conflicts between parent, child, and state arise—an understanding of past issues will provide a basis for more equitable decisions.

SAFE AND SOUND:
A CHILD'S RIGHT TO PROTECTION

Principle: The Child Shall Be Protected Against
All Forms of Neglect, Cruelty and Exploitation.
UN Declaration of the
Rights of the Child, 1989

Elisa Izquierda was born in New York on February 11, 1989, with cocaine in her bloodstream. She was given to her father either after she was abandoned by her mother at the hospital or removed by a social worker. She attended school regularly. Elisa thrived under her father's care—the only signs of trouble came after visits with her mother, when bruises appeared on her body and emotional upsets were frequent. In May 1994, Elisa's father died of cancer. Her mother received temporary custody. Even though Elisa stopped going to school regularly under her mother's care, and her mother had previously been reported to several child-abuse agencies, the

When the crown prince of Greece visited her school, Elisa's smile and her request that he take her away with him prompted the prince to offer to pay for all of her schooling.

judge assigned to the case gave Elisa's mother permanent custody of the child.

Elisa's teachers in her school, in New York City, noticed that she walked strangely and was withdrawn. They called the state child-abuse hot line and talked directly with the New York City Child Welfare Administration. Social workers who visited Elisa at home "saw no trouble." Yet, six months later, six-year-old Elisa was found dead, in her mother's apartment, from a blunt impact wound. She had been sexually abused, and her body was covered with cigarette burns. One of her finger bones protruded through her skin. Her mother told the police that she hit Elisa because the child was screaming, banging on the door, and "acting up." On July 31, 1996, Awilda Lopez, Elisa's mother, was sentenced to fifteen years to life for killing her daughter.

Public reaction to Elisa's death was that of shock, disbelief, and sadness. The questions raised were familiar. They are heard every time the media publicize a shocking child-abuse case. How could this have happened? Why wasn't something done to prevent this tragedy? Who was responsible? What went wrong?

The questions remained unanswered. Section 422 of the New York social services law, echoing similar federal and state laws around the country, prohibits any disclosures about child-abuse cases. This law was enacted in the interests of protecting the privacy of the child and the family, and in some instances it serves its purpose. For instance, families who are healing from the wounds resulting from a history of child abuse may not want any public interference or disruption during this process. However, in some cases like Elisa's the law actually works to the child's detriment. In these instances the law is used to hide flaws in the child-protection system and to shield abusers.

History Is Repeated. After Elisa's death, State Assembly Speaker Sheldon Silver said, "These are difficult times in this area, and the focus has to be on the rights of the children."[1] Sentiments similar to this were heard more than a hundred years before when the case of Mary Ellen McCormick, a physically abused foster child, was revealed to the public. Five-year-old Mary Ellen had spent her life locked either in a bedroom or a closet. She was never allowed outside and was whipped with a strip of rawhide if she did not work hard enough. When her plight was discovered by a social worker in 1873, there was no agency with the jurisdiction to remove children from a foster home. But there was an agency for animals—the SPCA, or the Society for the Prevention of Cruelty to Animals. On the grounds that Mary Ellen was a member of the animal kingdom, and was being treated cruelly, the SPCA rescued her from her foster home and started her on a new life. (Mary Ellen later married and successfully raised her own children.) In response to this case, the New York Society for the Prevention of Cruelty to Children was founded to provide legal support for abused children.

Child-Abuse Laws. It is cause for concern that one hundred years after Mary Ellen's case so many children continue to be victims of abuse. Despite the presence of laws and social-service agencies created to protect children from abuse, a report from the National Committee to Prevent Child Abuse estimates that 1,215 children died from abuse in 1995.

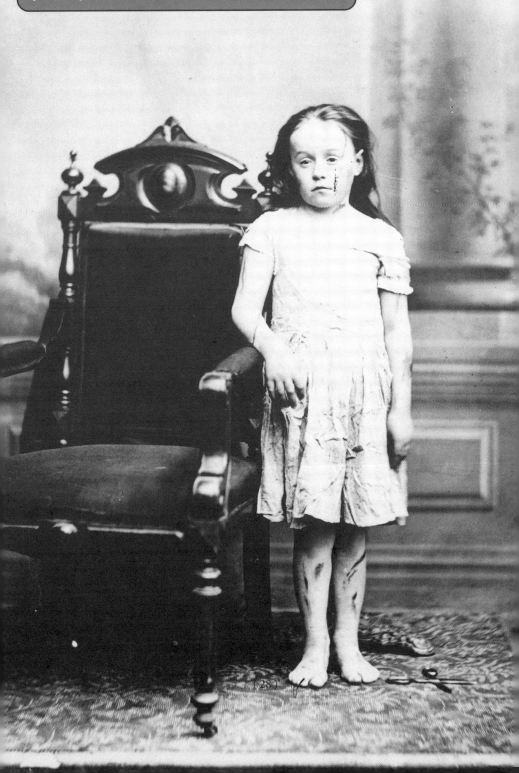

Mary Ellen McCormick, whose plight inspired the founding of the New York Society for the Prevention of Cruelty to Children

(28)

Children have the right to be free from neglect and physical abuse. The infliction of pain and suffering on a child by a child's custodian—whether a parent, relative, or a baby-sitter—is a punishable criminal offense. A system of support for abused children is in place under civil laws as well. The child herself can report this abuse to a trusted adult friend, teacher, or relative or call the telephone operator and ask to be connected to the state child-abuse hot line. Calling 911 when a child feels in immediate danger of being seriously injured by an adult should bring prompt help from the police. When the alleged abuse is brought to the attention of the state child-protective services, the complaint is investigated. If an emergency situation exists where a child is in danger of serious physical harm, the child can be removed from the home and placed in a foster home, pending a hearing before a judge. If the court determines that the situation can be remedied by providing help and support services to the parents and the family, the child will be returned home and the case will continue to be monitored. If the danger of continuing child abuse still exists, the child will remain in a foster home. A reunification plan is arranged by the judge with the family and the child-protection services. If these conditions are met, the child will be returned to the parents.

Reporting Child Abuse. Any citizen, children included, can report child abuse to a state protective or law-enforcement agency. Doctors, school officials, and other professionals are required by law to report suspected child abuse. But problems arise with follow-up procedures and accountability. In Harlem, the desperate cry of a fourth grader, written in an essay, "When I was eight my father raped me," was ignored. Only when the child told her grandmother about the incident was the father arrested.

Sometimes the fear of making an unfounded complaint prevents someone from reporting a suspected case of child abuse. A teacher in New York City, testifying before the Commission on Child Abuse and Neglect, said that the fear of angry retribution from parents accused of abuse makes school officials ignore mandatory reporting laws.

In some instances the complaint may prove to be unfounded, resulting in severe suffering and hardship for the parents. Parents of a seven-month-old experienced a nine-month "legal nightmare" after their child was taken to a hospital with a head injury. The parents told the doctor that the child had struck his head on a rattle during a fall. The doctor, who operated on a torn artery and a blood clot swelling in the child's brain, accused them of causing the injuries by shaking the baby. Under the close scrutiny of the social-service agency and the court, the parents had to surrender legal custody of their child to the grandmother and for nine months were not allowed to be alone with him. The family court judge finally exonerated them, finding that the evidence did not support "shaken baby syndrome" and ruling that the county could not take the child from his parents and put him in foster care. The parents paid $60,000 in legal fees and even considered leaving their community where they felt they would be living under a "shadow of suspicion."[2]

The issue here is whether saving the life of one child outweighs the problems and inconveniences to a family wrongly accused as a result of a strictly enforced reporting system.

Family Preservation and Protection. The Federal Adoption Assistance and Child Welfare Reform Act of 1980 states that federal funding of state programs is contingent upon states making reasonable efforts at keeping families together before removing the child to a foster home. Family preservation programs can help by providing counseling, emergency shelters, food, clothing, parental training, and treatment for drug addiction. The goal is to remove the risk of harm to the child, instead of removing the child. In cases where the child is removed, some programs provide the biological parents with visitation rights and transportation assistance while the child is in foster care in order to promote reunification. "The difference with family preservation," says one social worker in San Diego, "is we look for the strengths in people instead of focusing on their weaknesses, as the system always did before."[3] The underlying belief in this approach is that "the state can be a custodian and not a parent,"[4] and that the best hope for children lies with their own families.[5] There is an economic benefit to keeping families intact. The Center for the Study of Social Policy estimates that the average cost of family preservation services for a child in New York City is $5,000, compared with $13,500 per year for foster care.

Those who disagree with the focus on family preservation say that this approach puts the child's safety and well-being at risk. The alternative of placing a child in foster care, however, has its own risks. Craig Levine, a lawyer for Children's Rights Inc. (an organization established by the American Civil Liberties Union in the mid-1970s to assist children being cared for by the state), feels that a swing away from family preservation toward foster care will not provide all the answers. "Given the way the foster care system is running in New York City these days, the idea of putting kids into foster care to save them is to stretch the definition of 'save' about as far as Webster would permit," he says.[6]

Private organizations like Children's Rights Inc. and Lawyers for Children keep a watchful eye on government agencies in charge of protecting children. They bring any problems in the state system to the public's attention and try to resolve these problems with the assistance of the court. In New York a class-action suit (a lawsuit involving a number of plaintiffs with the same complaint) was brought on behalf of abused children who have been victimized by the city's Child Welfare Agency, which deals with issues like foster care. The lawyers would like the court to take over the agency, which has been described as the most dysfunctional and expensive in the country, and appoint a receiver to supervise it. In Washington, D.C., Children's Rights Inc. litigated the restructuring of the child-welfare system, which was so disorganized that it failed to claim $31 million allotted to it by the federal government.

The state of Illinois is proposing legislation to prevent people who have abused their children from receiving funds through preservation programs. Complaints from the ACLU state that the bill is anti-women, because most single parents are women, but Patrick Murphy, the writer of the bill, says that "any woman who stands by when the boyfriend beats the kid doesn't deserve the kid. You can't preserve a family that doesn't exist."[7]

Privacy or Disclosure? Would Elisa's case have had a different outcome if the child-welfare agency, and the court, had been open to public scrutiny? In a highly publicized case in Florida, reporter Tim Roche tracked the progress of a child, Charlotte May Puffinberger, after her stepsister, aged three and a half, was killed by Charlotte's father. The father was sentenced to ten years in prison, and the mother to nine months for not reporting the abuse. When the mother was released, she tried to regain custody of Charlotte. Roche reported on all the developments in Charlotte's case, including quoting fifty-four words from the judge's confidential decision granting custody of Charlotte to her foster mother. He refused to divulge his source and was cited for contempt of court. (He was sentenced to jail for disobeying a judge in the courtroom.) But his writing about the case fed the public's interest and turned the spotlight on how it was being handled. Charlotte's foster mother, Gayle Swift, said, "People need to know that people that cared about Charlotte felt that his actions served her well."[8]

Should the laws regarding confidentiality be changed? Illinois, Texas, Kentucky, Massachusetts, South Carolina, and Maryland have laws that have loosened the privacy constraints of child-abuse cases. "Elisa's law," passed recently in New York, and similar laws proposed in Connecticut and New Jersey, will ensure that abuse records are saved and made available to caseworkers, police, and others working on custody issues, in the hope that patterns of abuse can be detected more easily. "Confidentiality laws should not be allowed to mask accountability," says Joseph L. Bruno, the New York Senate majority leader. "It is precisely that lack of accountability that continues to place children like Elisa at risk."[9]

The New York Civil Liberties Union plans to challenge the law on the grounds that it fails to protect the privacy of those who are wrongfully accused. They fear that journalists will turn information about abuse cases into public knowledge.

On the flip side of the issue, a new law titled "Megan's law" is being challenged for violating the privacy rights of the abuser. Megan was the victim of a brutal murder by her neighbor. The child's parents lobbied the U.S. Congress to pass this law, which tracks the residences of convicted child abusers and molesters and provides the public with such information upon request. Megan's parents feel that Megan might be alive today if they knew about the danger that existed in their neighborhood. Civil liberties lawyers feel that a person who has served his sentence for his crime should have the right to start a new life with his right to privacy restored.

Children Against Child Abuse. Even with the immense strides taken since the time when Mary Ellen was rescued, the climate for encouraging children to report and punish abusers in some situations can be chilling. The fear that no one will believe them, or the possibility of further punishment, prevents children from reaching out for help. Under the Sixth Amendment, the accused has the right to confront his accuser in court, an intimidating situation for most children. In order to protect the child from this potentially traumatizing experience, the state of Maryland allows the child to be questioned in court through one-way closed-circuit television. In the case of *Maryland* v. *Craig* (1990), the U.S. Supreme Court found that the state's interest in protecting the psychological well-being of child-abuse victims may be sufficiently important to outweigh, in some instances, a defendant's right to face-to-face confrontation. Justice

Antonin Scalia disagreed. He believed that the objective of the state law was not primarily to protect the child but to get more convictions of guilty defendants.

Desiray Bartak, sexually abused by her godfather, won her case despite her own father's skepticism and taunts by fellow students. On a visit to Washington, D.C., at the invitation of First Lady Hillary Clinton, she said, "I want to inspire kids—to let other kids know that they are not alone."[10] Desiray also filed a civil suit against her godfather to compensate her for physical and emotional abuse, and she won. With her mother, she founded Children Against Rape and Molestation, a non-profit organization based in California. She writes a newsletter for abuse victims. She has appeared on the *Oprah Winfrey* and *20/20* television shows, spreading her message to other kids who are victims of abuse. She urges these kids to file a police report and keep on telling their story until someone listens to them. "I think a lot of children in her position are on the defensive mode," says her attorney Gloria Allred. "It has helped her [Desiray] to know that there are steps she can take to fight back, and to let other children know that there are steps they can take. I feel children need a spokesperson who is one of their own. I felt she would be someone who other children would be inspired by, so they could find their courage."[11]

Children are finding their voice, as the next chapter illustrates. Children are learning to protect their own interests by choosing to live in not only a safe environment but a happy and nurturing one as well.

IN THE CHILD'S BEST INTEREST

*You have a right to certain things. You have a
right to be cared for, to be educated. You have a
right to be loved.*[1]

Jeanette Laws, foster mother

Gregory Kingsley, age twelve, knew what he wanted. He
wanted, in his words, "a place to be happy, to feel safe,"
and finally, "just to be." During the previous eight years,
he had lived with his mother only seven months. What
he remembered were fights between his parents, his
father's heavy drinking, eviction by sheriffs, and too many
foster homes. "I had to take Gregory down to HRS
(Health and Rehabilitative Services) with his little suit-
case," said Rachel, his biological mother, the last time
she turned him over to the state of Florida. "He handled
it like a little man, but he didn't want to leave me."[2]

First Gregory was put in foster care, then in the state-
run Lake County Boys' Ranch. His mother never vis-

ited, called, or wrote to him. "I just thought she forgot about me," he said. Only three years earlier Gregory, with the knowledge of the law beyond his years, had filed a neglect-and-abuse charge against his father, with whom he was then living, in order for his mother to gain custody. But Rachel had married at seventeen and was a high-school dropout. She made $2.15 an hour plus tips as a waitress. With no child support, she could not pay her bills. She lost her phone, her electricity, and her apartment, and finally had to turn Gregory back to the state.

Gregory was at the ranch when George Russ, an attorney, came for an official visit. "I have eight children of my own," Russ said. "I was not looking for another child...but I couldn't get him off my mind."[3] On his second visit to the Russ home, Gregory asked if he could stay "forever and ever." His new family was ready to adopt him, but his biological mother wanted him back.

Custody Rights of Parents. Gregory knew he had two choices. He could go back to his natural mother and hope the state would step in and find him a permanent home if he was abandoned again. He had little faith in the system, however, as he had already been allowed to languish in foster care for nearly twice as long as the eighteen months allowed by state law. Or he could wait for a court-appointed attorney—one obligated to act in the "best interests" of the child but not necessarily in keeping with the child's wishes—to take his case to court. (A court-appointed attorney, or guardian *ad litum*, is obligated to act in the way he or she perceives is in the best interests of the child.) Also, the law clearly protects the right of biological parents to have custody over their children. The Supreme Court has ruled that "the custody, care and nurturing of the child resides first in the parents."[4] It is a right based on the presumption that parents as adults have the required qualities to bear a child and mold him or her in accordance with their beliefs as they see fit. No third party, including the state, may interfere with this fundamental right and force a family apart unless a child's personal safety is being threatened. Although Gregory's father signed away his legal claim to Gregory, his mother did not. She claimed she had surrendered Gregory temporarily because of poverty and would get him back when her circumstances improved. Gregory knew he needed a third option. "What can I say so the judge won't send me back?" Gregory asked his foster father.

"I told him," answered Russ, "that in my opinion he is a citizen of the United States, and that there are certain rights that citizens have: equal protection under the law, due process of law, access to the courts, the pursuit of happiness, and the right to an attorney of (one's) own choosing."[5]

Severing Family Ties. A few days later Gregory hired his own attorney, Jerri A. Blair of Orlando, Florida, to represent him in a formal and independent manner in a court of law. Gregory wished to sever legal ties with his biological parents—to "divorce" his parents, which is what made the news. The historic and far-reaching consequence, however, was that Judge Thomas S. Kirk, who ruled on the case, agreed that Gregory had the same constitutional right as an adult to protect his own interests, and he let him bring the suit with the lawyer of his own choice. The judge based his decision on the Florida state

Gregory Kingsley at age twelve on the witness stand.
There were some light moments, but the trial was
serious business for Gregory and the legal community.

constitution, which says that all natural persons have access to the courts and the legal rights that accompany them, including legal representation. "The most socially significant thing about that step," said Blair, "is that it allowed a child access to court to protect himself when the state failed to do so."[6]

Gregory won his case. His new name is Shawn Russ, and his new parents gave him a shirt emblazoned with the number 9—their ninth child. The journalist Anna Quindlen described this result as a step toward releasing the child from being a victim in society that "demands...young children sacrifice for the sake of what is best for their parents [when] it is supposed to be the other way around."[7]

Some child advocates are less inclined to place all the blame on parents. They believe that if states would comply with the Adoption Assistance and Child Welfare Act of 1980 and provide support and assistance to parents like Gregory's, situations like these would not arise.

Impact of the Gregory K. Ruling. Legal scholars continue to debate the impact of the Gregory Kingsley case. "What this...will mean is that more children will have certain rights that they didn't have before," claimed George Russ. "It will do what has been done for every other disenfranchised, powerless group. It will give them power."[8] Howard Davidson, director of the American Bar Association's Center on Children and the Law, is more conservative in his assessment. "The case clearly sends a message to parents that they are not free to neglect and mistreat children without consequence." But he added, "I don't think it is realistic to expect that the Gregory K. case is going to lead to large numbers of children having available to them, in any practical sense, a new remedy. Hopefully, though, it will mobilize those attorneys involved in juvenile court to try to do a better job on behalf of their clients."[9]

Shortly after the Kingsley case, in a custody suit in New York, an eleven-year-old boy was given the right to fire a court-appointed lawyer and hire another lawyer of his choosing. The judge, Justice William Rigler, said he wanted to ensure that the child was "comfortable with his lawyer and that there were no appearances of conflict."[10] According to Professor Martin Guggenheim [the child's chosen attorney], the boy was "extremely intelligent, articulate and sensitive" and had "a keen understanding of the subtleties of the dispute between his parents and a strong sense of being wronged and misused by this action."[11]

Legal scholars are not optimistic that the Kingsley decision will dramatically change the legal status or strengthen the legal rights of about 400,000 other children now in foster care. In March 1992, a few months before the Kingsley suit was resolved, the U.S. Supreme Court indicated its resistance to expanding the rights of children in Gregory's situation by not allowing foster-care children in Chicago to bring a suit that might have reformed the critically deficient system that was endangering their welfare. This was in keeping with its 1989 decision barring Joshua de Shaney's suit against the state of Wisconsin. Joshua, age four, suffered permanent brain damage when his father beat him. The boy had been returned to his father's custody despite the state's knowledge of his father's previously reported abuses.

Finally, the most newsworthy element of Gregory's case was undermined when the Florida appeals court disagreed with Justice Kirk's decision to allow Gregory to file his own case. The decision allowing the severance was not affected, however, since Gregory was joined later in his suit by George Russ and the Florida Social Services Agency.

What has emerged from the Kingsley case is a viable third voice, one crying out for the right of the child to be heard and considered in a legal proceeding that decides his or her future.

"There is a psychological difference in having a child speak in his own voice," says Elizabeth Bartholet, a Harvard law professor. "It is easier to forget the child's best interests if we don't allow the child to speak."[12]

Family Values at Risk. Critics of the Gregory Kingsley decision argue that it signals a dangerous movement to put the courts in the middle of family values. First Lady Hillary Clinton came under similar attack for the ideas she espoused in a 1973 article in the *Harvard Educational Review.* She stated that all minors are not incompetent and that mature older children should be legally empowered. Children's-rights advocates do not feel that this decision or Mrs. Clinton's proposals spell the demise of family values, nor do they envision an outbreak of children starting legal actions on their own. Instead, a child's right to independent legal representation would protect the child's interest, rather than only the interest of the parent or state. This could mean that a child could use that voice to keep a family together (as in cases where a parent may refuse to see the child or when the state might want to remove the child) as well as to break ties to his or her family.

In just such a case, Dan Weber, a Nebraska teenager who has had no contact with his family or his sister for three years, is seeking visitation rights with his sister.

His parents left him in the care of the state when he was fourteen because, in their words, he was "incorrigible." His grandmother was given custody of him and publicly criticized her daughter's actions. Dan asked the court to intervene and give him the right to be with his family. The deputy county attorney supports Dan's claim and argued his case before the Nebraska Supreme Court. Although his parents want to terminate their parental rights, Dan says he would like to reconcile with them. "I'm willing to. They need to be willing, too. I'd like to be able to talk to them, have a relationship with them."[13]

An example of a court intervention that did not bring the desired result for any of the parties was the case of Kimberly Mays. Kimberly, a fourteen-year-old girl from Florida, was switched at birth with another baby in the hospital, which she learned about when she was twelve years old. Her biological parents, Ernest and Regina Twigg, and her siblings wanted visitation rights, saying that the Mays had orchestrated the switch to ensure they had a healthier child (the other child died of a congenital heart defect). Kimberly petitioned the Florida court to break all ties with her biological family stating that she wanted to be left alone to live with the only father she knew. She got her wish. However, some months later she ran away from her father's home because he was "too strict." When she returned, it was to the Twigg's home. But not for long. When she refused to obey them, they placed her in a youth shelter for runaways.

Kimberly is now married. Her adoptive father gave her away at the wedding in early 1997. "I'm so happy; now I really feel I can start my life over," she said.

In this case, involving two sets of parents embroiled in a situation where the child's best interests were lost in an adult power struggle, the judge had to decide what to do. Consequently, a troubled teenager was given the responsibility to choose the best home for herself, which for her meant the home with the least rules. In a break from tradition, the wishes of the child were placed over the rights of the biological parents.

Minors Choose. The idea that the Gregory Kingsley case would advance the belief that a child's interest may not always be the same as that of his biological or adoptive parents was recently taken up in two cases. The court responded to these children's pleas in circumstances where their physical and emotional welfare was in extreme danger.

In 1995, Sonya Kinney, a deaf fifteen-year-old girl, wanted her sign-language interpreter to be her guardian, stating that her parents, who are divorced, had refused to learn sign language. Sonya's father's excuse was that he felt guilty about her disability. Her mother felt that Sonya should develop her speaking skills. In a further development, Sonya was removed from her mother's home because of contentions that she was being sexually abused by her stepfather. The judge ruled that her parents' failure to learn sign language prevented Sonya from communicating her fears about her stepfather, and he awarded custody of Sonya to her sign-language interpreter. "I'm saved. You saved me," Sonya said.[14]

In a second case, Liz from New York City, who was adopted as an infant, was placed in foster care after her adoptive mother had been accused of abusing her. Although Liz was happy in her foster home, her adoptive mother went to family court to have her removed from the foster home on the grounds that the foster family practiced a different religion from Liz's. (New York social-services law recommends that when practicable a child should be placed with a foster family of the same religion as the child.) The judge ruled in favor of the adoptive mother. Liz was placed in other foster homes, and finally, on the basis of a petition by her adoptive mother to the Child Welfare Administration, she was put into a psychiatric facility. Between her stays in foster homes, Liz lived on the streets. In a desperate cry for help, she appealed to a television news reporter to air her story. One attorney responded to her plea and agreed to take her case free of charge. Liz fought to return to her foster family, stating: "It is the one place I know where there is love, and I know I can just be a kid. That's really all I want. I'm just afraid that by the time I get there I won't be a kid anymore."[15] Although Liz's adoptive mother tried to regain custody, Liz's attorney was able to persuade the court not to return Liz to her. According to her attorney, Liz now lives in a group home and maintains a good relationship with her foster mother.

The Best Interest Identified. The Gregory Kingsley case has been described by some as "the precursor of the laws, catching up with society's evolution, from a time when children were considered chattel and parents were absolute."[16]

Although in the twentieth century protective legislation has been enacted in areas of child abuse, education, and child labor, the case of Gregory Kingsley highlights the predicament a child is in when both his or her parents and the state fail in their duty to protect what is in the best interests of that child. Who stands up for the child? The point is not that children can now divorce their parents because they are not permitted to go out on Friday night but that it is the right of every child to a safe, secure, happy childhood. The point is that if a child is part of a caring family which develops out of "biological, adoptive, foster, or common-law adoptive ties [where] the adults are the psychological parents and the children are wanted...the balanced opportunities for a unique development and for social adaptation are maximized."[17]

Article 3 of the United Nations Convention, an international legal guide for children's rights, states that the best interests of the child shall be a primary consideration in all judicial and administrative actions concerning children, and that a child capable of forming his or her own views shall have the opportunity to be heard in judicial and administrative proceedings. Article 18 states that parents and guardians must make the best interests of the child their basic concern. By signing this covenant, governments such as the United States agree not to pass any laws or take any action that is in contravention of the treaty. The terms of the treaty can be introduced in courts of law in the United States, not as binding law but as dicta, or information for the court to consider in making its decision.

Children are beginning to be heard. Judges are listening to children in custody disputes, and attorneys are striving to represent a child's interest when it is an issue. Legal organizations and social agencies are recognizing a duty to protect minors and are tuning into their concerns and wishes. In a book, *The Heart Knows Something Different*, James Knight, age twenty, and several others who spent much of their childhood in foster care, are finally given the chance to speak out about their needs and dreams. "Their writings," Knight says, "are an untapped source of insight into a system that exists for their safety but routinely ignores their advice."[18] Cases such as Gregory Kingsley's indicate how the law is evolving. If a child must rely on an adult to make a legal decision for him or her, the child's role is no longer a passive one. Now a child can actively work toward a legal solution that considers his or her voice, rather than only the voices of the parents or state.

CHAPTER FOUR

FREE TO BE ME: FIRST AMENDMENT PROTECTIONS

Give me liberty to know, to utter and to argue
freely according to conscience, above all liberties.
John Milton, *Areopagitica,* 1644

Paul K. Kim, a senior at Newport High School, Bellevue, Washington, had a 3.88 grade point average. He scored 1510 on his Scholastic Achievement Test. He was a National Merit finalist, with a chance to receive a $2,000 college scholarship. He felt confident applying to schools like Harvard, Stanford, and Columbia.

In February of his senior year, Paul followed the long-held senior tradition of lampooning his school by joking that his classmates "majored in football" and were "preoccupied with sex." He meant to poke fun. But Paul was also a computer buff and he took his lampoon one step further—he published it on the Internet's World Wide Web, calling it the "Unofficial Newport High School Home Page." Then he linked the page to Internet sites that offered sexually explicit material.

Anyone surfing the net could come across the "Unofficial Newport High School Home Page" and, through that, click onto articles about sex and even onto a picture of a *Playboy* centerfold. Paul included a disclaimer that "no one associated with the school" was responsible for the page, other than himself, and he signed his name.

When word of Paul's page reached the school administration, the principal withdrew her endorsement of him as a National Merit finalist. After that, and without Paul's knowledge, she faxed letters to the seven universities he had applied to. She told the schools that she could no longer support any recommendations his high school teachers may have given the universities, and that she would no longer support him for a National Merit Scholarship.

Although the principal told Paul about her letter regarding the National Merit finalists, he learned about the faxes to the colleges when Columbia's admissions department asked him for an explanation. Paul's parents were divorced, he lived with his mother, and money was tight. He needed financial aid, but most of all he needed an acceptance from one of the schools. "She (the principal) told me what I had done was immoral. I cried in front of her and told her she was destroying everything I had worked so hard for,"[1] said Paul.

Paul wrote letters of appeal to the school district, asking for another chance at the scholarship and then turned to the American Civil Liberties Union (ACLU). The ACLU argued that the principal had violated Paul's First Amendment right to free speech. Also, by failing to inform Paul that she had written to the college admissions officers, his Fourteenth Amendment right to due process was violated. The ACLU threatened the school administrators with a lawsuit if they continued to withhold their support.

Lucy Helm, one of Paul's ACLU attorneys, said that Paul had created a "humorous electronic newspaper" on what is an uncensored and easily accessible information superhighway, and that he was within his First Amendment rights to do so. Citing a federal court decision of 1988, when high school students in Washington State could not be disciplined for circulating an underground newspaper, even though school administrators feared possible disturbances or embarrassment, the ACLU helped Paul to press charges. "People in authority," Paul Kim said, "shouldn't be able to enforce their own morality on others."[2]

Freedom of Speech and Obscenity. The Paul Kim case is believed to be the first ACLU case on the Internet involving both a minor and freedom of speech. Freedom of speech is the liberty to speak and write without fear of government restraint. It is protected by the First Amendment. In other words, citizens have the right to comment, complain, disagree with, protest, and even lampoon commonly held community beliefs and government policies. The restraints on these freedoms are explicitly defined by laws and court rulings. Speech that is obscene, incites violence, or recklessly and maliciously damages another person's name is subject to exclusion from this protection.

Traditionally, the First Amendment rights of young people, especially in the area of obscenity, have been more limited than those of adults. Unlike adults, minors have no legal right to possess obscene materials, such as books, magazines, and videos, even in their own homes. State laws prohibit minors from purchasing these materials. Even wider discretion has been given by the courts to school authorities in limiting free speech rights within the school.

But what about rules in cyberspace? Will traditional rules and standards have to be revised to conform to "the communications medium for the 21st century?"[3]

The groundbreaking issues in Paul Kim's case will not be decided by a court of law because he reached an out-of-court settlement in his favor. The school issued a statement saying that their students should not be punished for free speech. On the chance that Paul would have received the scholarship, the school gave him $2,000, and he was reinstated as a National Merit finalist. Paul is now at the university of his choice.

No doubt these issues and others like them will surface more often in the future, since the Internet has been described as "the most important thing that has happened to communications since the printing press."[4] The question of whether the courts will respect freedom of the Net as much as they do freedom of the press was answered by the Supreme Court in June, 1997. The ACLU and several giant computer companies successfully challenged the constitutionality of the Communications Decency Act, which regulates the dissemination of indecent material on the Internet in the interests of protecting children from pornography.

The Court agreed that government control of the Internet is wrong, that people should have the right to free access without government interference. If there is a problem, the parents should handle it. Others still disagree, believing that the only way to protect children from pornography is through laws regulating it.

History. "Freedom of speech is something that we will always have to fight for, and there will be those who want to silence others. Freedom of speech is an issue every day; you work for it every day in small conversations you might have with your friends or in a speech you might make on a political issue."[5] Mary Beth Tinker said this twenty years after she, at age fifteen, and her thirteen-year-old brother John, fought their school board for the right to wear black armbands to protest the war in Vietnam.

The armbands were approximately 3 inches (8 centimeters) wide and were stamped in the center with the white peace symbol. In December 1965, a group of students in Des Moines, Iowa, wore them to school. By doing this, they expressed a political opinion, known as "symbolic speech." When the otherwise peaceful protest was banned by the administration, all but three students removed the bands—the Tinker youths and sixteen-year-old Christopher Eckhardt. Represented by lawyers from the ACLU, Mary Beth, John, and Christopher challenged the ban against the bands on the grounds that it violated their First Amendment right to express their opinion, and that it discriminated against them as students, a Fourteenth Amendment violation.

The case went to the U.S. Supreme Court, and four years later, by a vote of 7–2, the Court decided in favor of the students. Justice Abe Fortas wrote the historic majority opinion. What he said has often been quoted: "It can hardly be argued that neither students nor teachers shed their rights at the schoolhouse gate.... students in school as well as out of school are 'persons' under our Constitution."[6]

Claiming that the armbands might cause a disturbance was not a strong enough reason to ban them. The Court went on to argue that even though any word and departure from "absolute regimentation" could cause a problem, according to the Constitution that is an acceptable risk.

This was the first time that free-speech protection, guaranteed under the First Amendment, was extended to students in school. It became a landmark case, one that would change how the Constitution could be interpreted in the future.

Like most landmark decisions, the Tinker ruling fostered a great deal of discussion. Although a supporter of free speech, Justice Hugo Black dissented, stating that although the freedom to express ideas is unconditional, the right to express them any time and any place should be restricted. Schools should not "surrender control of the American public school students," he said.[7]

The next decade and a half left the Tinker decision unchallenged. Minor conflicts were settled out of court, such as a complaint by a teacher at a junior high school in Arlington, Virginia, that students wearing the fashionable pea coat, a standard Navy issue, were showing disrespect for Navy veterans. This was set against the background of the Vietnam War, an era of heightened awareness about the justifications for the war. It was resolved out of court by allowing students to bring the coats to their lockers, but not allowing the coats to be worn in school.

It appeared that the Tinker case had set a precedent that would go unchallenged. But in 1983, journalism students at Hazelwood East High School near St. Louis, Missouri, wrote an article for the school newspaper about three students who were pregnant, and a second article

Many First Amendment violations have been challenged successfully by junior high and high school students. However, when students at Lost Creek Elementary School in Indiana challenged their principal for banning T-shirts carrying the slogans "I Hate Lost Creek," "Racism," and "Unfair Grades," the students lost. The 7th Circuit Court reasoned that the age of a student is a factor that can be used to determine if that student should have free-speech rights. In other words, younger students might not have the same rights of speech as older ones.[8]

about how a divorce could affect teenagers in a family. Although the students discussed in the articles were not named, the principal felt that everyone would be able to identify them. He said the subject matter was "inappropriate and unsuitable" for teenagers and stopped the press on two of the articles. The students, stating their First Amendment rights to freedom of speech and freedom of the press were being violated, took the case to court.

Five years later the Supreme Court decided that the students had no legal authority to print the articles because the paper belonged to the school, not the students. Unlike Paul Kim's Web page, Hazelwood East High School sponsored the paper, and the students were graded on their stories. The majority opinion of the Court was that since the goal of the paper was educational, the school could legally censor material it considered inappropriate.

Justice William Brennan, Jr., was one of the dissenters. Fearing that the decision would set the rights of students back to the days before the Tinker decision, he said school newspapers were as worthy of protection as the regular press. "The young men and women of Hazelwood East High School expected a civics lesson," Justice Brennan stated, "but not the one the Court teaches them today."[9]

Coded Yearbook Messages and Censorship. Although the right to publish in the United States is broad, it is not absolute. Restrictions usually occur when it is perceived that someone is being harmed.

In Greenwich High School, Connecticut, five senior boys slipped a coded message into their yearbook. In the captions below their pictures, the boys each spelled out a segment of the phrase "Kill the Niggers." The message was in alphabetical order by the boys' last names and was discovered when one of them bragged about the stunt. The teens were suspended from school for ten days and were barred from the graduation ceremonies, although they did receive their diplomas. They also had to spend three weeks in a "civil rights boot camp," visit Harlem in New York City, talk to Holocaust survivors, and read books about people with different ethnic backgrounds.

In effect, the students had used their yearbook, which represented 2,000 other students at the school, as well as the teachers and administration, to send messages of racial bigotry and hate. Clearly, their rights to free speech and freedom of the press took second place to the rights of others to be free from statements of prejudice and bigotry.

In this picture taken in 1965, Mary Beth Tinker and her brother John display the armbands that created a legal storm that went all the way to the U.S. Supreme Court.

Movie Censorship. What about cases of censorship in which the issues are not as easily defined as in the previous example? To avoid government regulation, movies are rated by voluntary agreement within the industry, but by whose standards? Usually the guideline is "prevailing community standards," but in a country as large and diverse as America, is it possible to draw such a distinction? Compliance with the ratings is voluntary as well—some theaters strictly enforce the system, while others leave it to the individuals selling the tickets. An R rating (children under 17 must be escorted by an adult) rarely stops a teenager from seeing a movie outside the classroom. Teachers showing R-rated movies in class for artistic or historical value have been fired or suspended. (One teacher was fired for showing the movie *Dead Poet's Society*, rated PG, to seventh graders.)

In March 1996, a judicial hearing officer ruled that a high school teacher in Littleton, Colorado, could not be fired for showing the R-rated movie *1900*, a four-hour film about the rise of fascism in Italy, which contained explicitly violent and sexual scenes. Because the community had no fixed policy on requiring parental permission to show R-rated movies, the teacher could not be fired. "It's an example of a great art film," said Alfred Wilder, the teacher. But Ron Mitchell, the principal, felt that "kids are a captive audience and they should not see the film because it contains several things that our community could find objectionable."[10] Parents and teachers in other states are petitioning for stricter controls on showing these R-rated movies in the classroom. New federal and state "parents' rights" legislation is being introduced (without much success), calling for more parental control on censorship issues in the school.

Music Ratings. Song lyrics are another gray area when it comes to censorship. In 1985, Tipper Gore, wife of Vice President Al Gore, and Susan Baker founded the Parents Music Research Center in an attempt to prod the record industry to self-censor the lyrics of their songs. This was nothing new. Church leaders in the nineteenth century routinely altered the librettos of Verdi's operas, in accordance with the political or sexual sensitivities of regional audiences. Songs by Stephen Foster, Billie Holiday, Bob Dylan, Crosby, Stills and Nash, and the Beatles, to name a few, have been banned for allusions to drugs, sex, and racism, although one song, "Transfusion," by Nervous Noruus, was banned because, according to a radio executive, "there's nothing funny about a blood transfusion."[11]

The ratings are voluntary and consist of a warning sticker on recordings deemed "explicit." Supporters of the system deny that labeling is censorship. They consider it a helpful guide for parents. But record store chains treat the stickered product differently. Some stores ask for proof of age, and others refuse to stock labeled music, even though, as in Verdi's day, audiences prefer the original versions. Who would be harmed if labeling were made a law—the record companies, whose sales might decrease; the artist, such as rappers who call themselves "street historians," whose creativity could be hampered; the child who might be denied access to new thoughts and sounds? Supporters feel that labeling is a small price to pay for protecting children from lyrics that glorify and, some say, promote violence, drug addiction, suicide, and brutality.

Censorship and Books. Are books immune from censorship? At some point, "book burning" has polarized the citizens of almost every society. In 1982, in *Board of Education, Island Trees Union Free School District* v. *Pico*, the Supreme Court supported school libraries as "environment(s) especially appropriate for the recognition of the First Amendment rights of students." Nine books, believed to be contrary to the values of the community, were removed earlier from library shelves by the school board. These volumes included *Slaughterhouse Five* by Kurt Vonnegut and *The Naked Ape* by Desmond Morris. After the Court ruling, they were allowed back on. Discretion to remove books "may not be exercised in a narrowly partisan or political manner," said the Court.[12]

This is a volatile issue, one that is debated in libraries, public and private, across the nation. The issue involved is the right of parents to raise their children according to their beliefs and their conscience versus First Amendment rights to preserve an "uninhibited marketplace of ideas in which truth will ultimately prevail."[13] History has shown that censorship of literature based on prevailing community standards of morality does not stand the test of time. As absurd as it may seem today, *The Wizard of Oz*, because it portrays "good witches," and *The Diary of Anne Frank*, because it asserts that all faiths are equally valid, and even the dictionary, because it contains such words as "bed" and "ass," were threatened with censorship in the past.

Today children's book authors are fighting censorship on a different level. Some publishers, in an attempt to not offend their intended market, self-censor pictures that might imply affection between people of the same sex or between adults and children (for example, they will not show pictures of children in bed with their parents).

Parents, by law, have the authority to determine what their children should read. In some instances, this control extends into the child's school. As long as the material is not prohibited by law, schools can decide whether to keep the offending book in or out of the curriculum. In Chappaqua, New York, parents objected to the blunt and explicit language in Magic Johnson's book *What You Can Do to Prevent Aids* used in their high school AIDS education curriculum. "I'm not a prude," said one parent, "and I think the children need education, but you can certainly question the way these things are taught."[14] The district dropped the book from its reading list.

School Prayer. Freedom of religion—the first freedom mentioned in the First Amendment—states that "Congress shall make no law respecting an establishment of religion or prohibiting the free exercise thereof." This means that the government cannot favor or "place its official stamp of approval" on one religion (the establishment clause), nor can the government interfere with an individual's practice of his or her chosen religion. The writers of the Constitution were particularly sensitive to protecting this liberty since the original colonists came to America from England and other parts of Europe to escape religious intolerance and persecution. The Supreme Court of the United States has interpreted this amendment to prohibit laws that force religion on students in public schools. Students in private schools can practice their religious beliefs, but not if that practice might have a discriminatory impact on another person. In this case, the First Amendment right to worship takes a back seat to the equal-protection right of the Fourteenth Amendment.

In 1925 the Scopes trial, one of the most famous in history, decided how students would learn about the origin of human beings. John Scopes wanted to teach his students the scientific theory of evolution promoted by Charles Darwin. This theory states that humans have evolved over hundreds of generations from more primitive life forms. Scopes challenged a Tennessee law that required teachers to teach the theory of Creationism (from the Book of Genesis, which states that the universe was created by God). He was convicted and fined $100. He appealed and won his case. Forty-three years later, the Supreme Court agreed that laws like the one in Tennessee were unconstitutional because they promoted a religious belief.

In 1948 the Supreme Court decided that the state of Illinois could not allow public schools to instruct children in religion in the classroom during school hours (*McCollum* v. *Board of Education*). In 1962, in the case of *Engel* v. *Vitale*, the Court struck down teacher-led classroom prayer by making unconstitutional a law giving school officials the option to mandate daily prayer. Thirty years later, graduation prayer led by a clergyman was also banned because it smacked of "establishment of religion."

An issue that has surfaced recently in public school is whether student-led prayer is illegal as well. Is this an issue of protecting a minor's right to free speech, or is it a novel way to introduce prayer into schools? Students at a Marshville, North Carolina, school tested this by challenging the school principal when he banned individual student speakers from expressing their religious views at their graduation ceremony. The students enlisted the aid of the American Center for Law and Justice, which helped them fight for their belief that student speakers should be allowed to include religious themes in the graduation program. "We fought to get what we thought was right," said the students, and their demands were met.[15] Although the American Civil Liberties Union has no problem with individual students airing their religious views, they still believe that it comes too close to violating the establishment clause and probably will not withstand a constitutional challenge.

This is a controversial issue that lawmakers have trouble leaving alone. Almost every year since 1962, a school-prayer amendment has been introduced in Congress, but none has been passed into law. In 1995, Representative Ernest Istook, Jr., of Oklahoma sponsored a school-prayer amendment that would permit religious expression, not compel it. "The decision of whether to have prayer at some kind of school activity should properly be made by the people that are involved in that activity, not by a federal judge, not by an ACLU attorney," he said. "This is a community decision, not a federal decision."[16]

Opponents feel that the amendment caters to protecting the rights of the majority. Rather than protecting religious liberty, which was one of the principles on which the United States was founded, this would be a first step toward creating a religion endorsed by the majority. This would be in direct violation of the "establishment clause" of the First Amendment.

Supporters of the school-prayer amendment believe that the establishment clause allows the government to discriminate against religious activity. These people believe that only a constitutional amendment can correct

the right to due process and equal protection under the law. In addition, "police are busy with serious crimes, and they don't have the time to play parent, [and] see if the youngster has a note from Mommy and Daddy," said ACLU spokesman Ed Martone, executive director of the New Jersey chapter.[20]

Most teenagers dislike the curfew law. "We're forced out of our own town," one complained.[21] Others feel that it is house arrest based only on age, and that people under eighteen should not have fewer rights than those over eighteen. Some also fear that minority teenagers will be picked up more often than others, leading to racial problems.

Residents of some New Jersey communities report an improved quality of life due to the curfew law. Car thefts are down, traffic is no longer in gridlock, boom boxes are off the streets, tires are less apt to be slashed. "It is a crime-stopping tool," said one area policeman of the new law.[22]

A new policy adopted by the largest mall in the world, the Mall of America in Bloomington, Minnesota, requires that anyone under the age of sixteen be escorted to the mall on Friday and Saturday nights by a "chaperone" who is over the age of twenty-one. Federal courts, in the past, have ruled that shopping malls are private spaces and therefore not subject to First Amendment rights, but state courts do not always take that position. California, for example, ruled that shopping centers have taken the place of the downtown, and therefore do come under First Amendment restrictions. Teenagers interviewed at the mall found the policy unfair because it punishes all young people, not just those who are causing problems.

The ACLU contends that parents, not the mall or the government, should decide if their children can go to the mall unattended. The issue here is whether keeping safety and order in America's malls for the majority of shoppers is more important than a child's right to be in a public space or a parent's right to decide when and with whom their child can go to a mall.

So far, the laws stand up to challenge if they are specific and focused. In 1987 the ACLU successfully challenged a curfew in Bordentown, New Jersey, that held parents as well as children responsible. The ordinance allowed police officers to "exercise reasonable judgment" in enforcing curfews. This wording was so broad that it was found to be unconstitutional. The new ordinance attempts to establish clear standards regarding the responsibility of both parents and children.

Children Should Be Seen and Not Heard. Children are not only seen and heard today, but are changing the laws of the country. Since the days of *Tinker* v. *Des Moines Independent School District*, students have had increased freedom to exercise one of the most important rights in our society—the right to express opinions freely and without fear of governmental interference. Not every challenge involving a child is upheld. Generally speaking, however, if a child's First Amendment rights are restricted without reasonable cause, the child's right stands. Parents have general veto power over how their children express themselves. Schools have rules that affect freedom of expression for the sake of keeping order. The state can restrict First Amendment freedoms, such as curfew and obscenity laws, on the basis of protection.

But the bottom line is that a minor is protected by First Amendment rights. These rights can be exercised to legally challenge anyone, except parents, from trying to unreasonably restrict the way children express their thoughts and ideas.

THE RIGHT TO PRIVACY

The human animal needs a freedom seldom mentioned, freedom from intrusion. He needs a little privacy quite as much as he wants understanding or vitamins or exercise or praise.
Phyllis McGinley, *The Province of the Heart: A Lost Privilege*

Brooke Shields grew up in the limelight. A model from the age of one, by the time she was an adolescent she had starred in several movies and her name was a household word. She was used to seeing her picture on magazine covers, on posters and billboards, and in the newspaper. In 1975 her mother, who was her manager, signed a contract on Brooke's behalf to have a series of photos taken of Brooke in a bathtub to "depict the woman in the little girl, to highlight the sensuality of the pre-pubescent youth."[1] Brooke was ten years old. The photos first appeared in a publication by Playboy

Press, and later two blowups were displayed in the window of the Charles Jourdan Salon on Fifth Avenue in New York City.

In 1980, when Brooke found out about the reprints of these photos in the French *Photo* magazine she was embarrassed by them. "I wasn't embarrassed when they were taken, but since then I've become more conscious of boys, of my body and myself. Now I just want to be myself. Those pictures are not me now," she said.[2] Shields filed an action in 1981 against the photographer for invasion of her right to privacy. The Court of Appeals in New York ruled that, because her success and public image were based on the exploitation of this "unique compound of innocence and sexuality," her privacy rights were not violated.[3] Also, her mother had signed a contract on her behalf. Although minors are not irrevocably held to contracts they might enter into, the judge determined that Shields could not break this contract. The only protection the court gave her was a warning to the photographer to be responsible in the future, and not allow the photos to be used in magazines "where the appeal is of predominantly prurient interest."

This case illustrates how a minor's right to privacy, in some instances, may be forfeited before he or she may feel the necessity to claim it. One judge on the case raised an important issue. Should a child be penalized for the questionable judgment of her parent? He pointed out that this type of unconscionable contract should be policed by the court in the interests of the child, whom he describes as "the hapless victim." Until the law is changed to provide for court approval in modeling contracts for minors that may involve nudity, "child models will have to rely on the good judgment of their parents or guardians."[4]

Legal Protections. The right to privacy, according to Supreme Court Justice Louis Brandeis, is "the right to be left alone—the most comprehensive of rights and the right most valued by civilized men."[5]

Although the right to privacy is not mentioned directly in the Constitution, the Fourth Amendment, which was added to the Constitution in 1791 as a protection against unreasonable search and seizure by the government, has been interpreted to protect a person's reasonable expectation of privacy. The need for this protection dates from the time when British officers, without warning or warrants, conducted searches for "smuggled goods" in the homes of the colonists.

The guarantee of this right has several sources. The Fourteenth Amendment, which states that no person will be denied life, liberty, or property without due process, has been interpreted by the Supreme Court as protecting the right of family members to make decisions within and about the family without state interference. The Fifth Amendment gives citizens the right to remain silent in situations where they may otherwise be forced to incriminate themselves. The First Amendment protects the right of persons to freely associate with individuals or groups of their choice without state interference. The Ninth Amendment, in a broad statement, gives people rights that are not specifically covered in the Constitution.

The constitutional amendments mentioned above set the boundaries for defining an individual's "personal space" by putting protections on certain rights, such as the right to remain silent. They also give the courts an outline in limiting actions that may infringe on another's rights. All of this ensures citizens "a reasonable expectation" of privacy. These constitutional protections are even further strengthened by state laws that must remain consistent with constitutional interpretations. The application of these protections is not clearly defined for minors, however, since their rights are filtered through the authority of parents and guardians and, when necessary, through the state itself, acting *in loco parentis* (in the place of the parent). A common example of *in loco parentis* is school officials acting within the school environment.

In today's legal climate, a child can expect his or her right to privacy to be limited in most instances. In 1995 the Supreme Court, in *Veronia School District* v. *Acton,* upheld this legal trend by approving blanket drug testing for school athletes. Explaining this limitation of a child's privacy rights, Justice Antonin Scalia stated that students should be "inculcated with the habits and manners of civility" and "protected from drug use and violent crime in schools [which] have become major social problems."[6]

Privacy in the Home. Practical day-to-day living in a family requires a mutual respect for the privacy needs of each member. However, as a child's role evolves in the eyes of the law and in society, parents struggle to maintain a balance between ensuring that their child is safe and respecting the child's need for privacy. Privacy within the family is still, therefore, a privilege to be earned by the adolescent by trust rather than an entitlement given by the law. Screening phone calls, censoring books, limiting television hours, and looking through their children's drawers, closets, and backpacks are all part of a parent's prerogative, and as long as the act does not amount to physical abuse, the extent of these activities is determined by parents and not by the law. Where most families stress safety over privacy, the balance that is achieved is often determined by the level of communication and understanding established in each family.

The reaction to a home drug-test kit that parents can use to detect the presence of drugs on the surface of a child's desk, books, or even on a football, shows the mixed feelings that this issue raises. The ACLU has reservations about the effect of the kit on parent/child relations, but otherwise has no legal quarrel with it. "Parents have the right to look through their kids' rooms," said Robyn Blumner, executive director of the ACLU in Miami.[7] Kristin Fay, a high school senior, thinks "it's an invasion of privacy. It shows a lack of trust. No one likes it when someone goes behind your back."[8] Adrian, a fourteen-year-old abuser of alcohol and other substances, took the opposite view. "It could be a way of helping out the kid," he said, "and finding out earlier and getting him help."[9]

Parents Guarding Privacy Rights. Parents are usually the first line of defense against governmental or public intrusions into their children's privacy, and they can often stop or deter violations. As shown by Brooke Shields's case, however, sometimes the child's right to privacy is forfeited by the parent only to be reclaimed later by the child. Whether raised by child or parent, more and more cases involving the privacy rights of children are coming to the forefront.

Fifteen-year-old Shaka King was returning home from a basketball game when he was forced into a police squad car and taken to the precinct station to be a filler in a lineup. His mother filed a suit against the City of New York. His lawyer demanded the return of any photos taken of Shaka at the precinct so that he would not be mistakenly identified in future cases. Minors can volunteer as fillers, but only with parental consent. Shaka's mother felt that both her custodial rights as a mother and her son's right to privacy were violated in this incident. The issue to be resolved here is whether a person's individual right to be left alone is more important than a particular method of combating crime.

Balancing Freedom of Speech and Privacy Rights. Intrusive actions by the media are becoming more frequent, and more blatant, with the growing popularity of magazine shows. A report in the *Miami Herald* related the story of a sixteen-year-old girl who called 911 during a suicide attempt. The sheriff's deputies came to her rescue, but a television crew for the show *Cops* also came along and televised the incident. Her parents filed a suit for invasion of privacy. She was scarred for life, said her family, because all of the girl's friends and acquaintances recognized her. Attorneys for the television network claimed that the report was of legitimate public interest and that they took precautions to safeguard the child's privacy by blurring her face while on screen. They also had received written permission from her sister to enter the house, but the sister contended that she did not know what she was signing. Was this a legitimate intrusion or was it exploitation, asked the girl's attorney. In other words, was this "news?" Was this situation important enough to the public to supersede the privacy right of a private citizen? The Supreme Court has given the press wide latitude in reporting "newsworthy" events involving private citizens. Even if a mistake is made about the facts, there is no liability unless the press acted in "reckless disregard of the truth." "Acting maliciously" is the benchmark for liability in reporting news about a public official, and unless these lines are crossed, the press may not be liable to the person whose reputation they may have damaged or whose privacy they may have invaded. The Supreme Court has stated that the risk of exposure of oneself to others "is an essential incident of life in a society which places a primary value on freedom of speech and press."[10] But the attorney for the girl on the *Cops* show argued that "people do not become public figures by way of calling 911."[11] In other words, the young woman did not seek out publicity by calling the police for help.

Perhaps Mark Twain sized up the situation best when he stated that "there are laws to protect the freedom of the press's speech, but none that are worth anything to protect the people from the press."[12]

Protective Laws. In March 1968 the U.S. Supreme Court, in *Ginsberg* v. *New York*, upheld a New York statute that prohibited the sale of magazines such as *Playboy* and *Penthouse* to minors. The Court commented that "parents...who have this primary responsibility for children's well-being are entitled to the support of laws designed to aid discharge of that responsibility." This responsibility, according to British sociologist Ronald Fletcher, is made especially difficult today because of the invasion of television into 98 percent of the homes in the Western world. In the past the fireplace was the center of the home, "with each family continually and cumulatively weaving its own private world."[13] According to Fletcher, today the focus in the home is the television set. Instead of children learning social awareness through exposure to the extended family and community values, this basic family group that centered around the hearth each evening to discuss the day's events now gathers around the television, which invades the home with "throngs of facts and values..."[14] The lack of this interactive family-centered time deprives children of developing a core of personal judgment to carry them successfully through life, says Fletcher. Newton Minow, former chairman of the Public Broadcasting System (PBS) and of the Federal Communications Commission (FCC) during the presidency of John F. Kennedy, states in his book *Abandoned in the Wasteland* that the strangers who enter our homes through the gateway of the family television set do so because the United States has left its children's television policy, insofar as it has one, to the discretion of the television industry. "But at the end of the day, the truth is that the strangers who dominate our children's lives can do so because we let them: parents, educators, foundations and public officials—all of us—have abandoned the nation's children to their care."[15] Some of the laws he describes are the Federal Communications Act of 1934 and the Children's Television Act of 1990. The former gives broadcasters free rein of the air waves so long as they "serve the public interest, convenience and necessity." The latter requires commercial broadcasters to include a few hours a week of educational and informational shows in their programming schedules for children. Minow recommends a more effective public policy that includes meeting the child's need to be prepared for life as a productive citizen, protecting the child from the harm that results from overexposure to violence, and providing parental support and education.

It is estimated that a child watches approximately 15,000 hours of television before finishing high school (4,000 more hours than in the classroom), and, according to the American Psychological Association, the average child witnesses 8,000 murders and 100,000 acts of violence on television before finishing elementary school.[16]

The issue then is what role the law should play in regulating a child's exposure to the media. Should the law determine who is responsible for monitoring and protecting the child, or should this determination be made by parents or broadcasters?

In response to the growing concern over programming and extensive lobbying for legislation to curb unsuitable television programs for children, President Bill Clinton recently signed the Telecommunications Reform Bill, which requires the installation of a "v" chip in all new television sets. This will allow parents to "turn off" the television when they do not want their children to watch something such as violent programs. This may be viewed as an infringement of First Amendment freedoms, or it may be interpreted as a step toward giving the family the right to decide what type of programming should enter the home. The Communications Decency Act, a part of this bill, also made it a crime to transmit indecent material over the Internet or online computer services if the material is accessible to children.

The act was being challenged in court by the ACLU, and by a bill in the Senate, for being too broad, and also for violating constitutionally protected free speech. Senator Patrick Leahy of Vermont, who introduced the bill to repeal the act, said, "Internet users will have to limit all language used and topics discussed to that appropriate for kindergartners, just in case a minor clicks into the discussion. No literary quotes from racy parts of *Catcher in the Rye* or *Ulysses* will be allowed."[17]

The Justice Department opposed the ACLU challenge, arguing that the benefits of protecting children from online pornographic images and speech is in the public interest. The mother of a fourteen-year-old from Mamaroneck, New York, may agree. A fifty-one-year-old pedophile from Seattle, Washington, posing as a thirteen-year-old boy, chatted over the Internet with her daughter until they had established an intimate relationship. He confessed to being older, and they agreed to meet in person. The girl's mother was able to intercept their liaison. When the offender was arrested, the police found that he had been in contact with more than twenty-five young people via the Internet. He is being charged in Seattle, Washington, with statutory rape, or having sex with a minor under the age of twelve.

On June 26, 1997 the United States Supreme Court decided that the law was unconstitutional. Justice John Paul Stevens wrote that freedom of speech under the first amendment had to be protected on the Internet in the same way it is protected in books and newspapers. This means that although indecent material may be protected, obscene material is not. The Supreme Court has defined obscenity as that which appeals to prurient, or lustful, interests.

The Supreme Court has also ruled that the right to privacy in the home does not extend to child pornography, and, in *Ginsberg* v. *New York*, that children's constitutional rights to freedom of expression are not violated by statutes that prevent them from exposure to obscene material. In 1978 the Supreme Court agreed with the FCC decision to fine the owners of a radio station that aired the "Seven Dirty Words" monologue by George Carlin. The Court was not convinced by the broadcaster's argument that the listener (in this case a father and son hearing it on a car radio) could have switched off the offensive program. Justice John Stevens wrote that First Amendment protections should be limited in the area of broadcasting because this form of communication is so accessible to children. Based on these precedents, the new law did not withstand a constitutional challenge.

The Court sent out a clear message that parents and guardians, not government, are responsible for controlling a minor's use of the Internet. Rather than leaving it up to providers to monitor material, parents can block a minor's access to certain web sites and chat rooms by choosing control options offered by all major on-line services or by installing software offered by companies like Vancouver, Canada's Net Nanny and Surf Watch of Los Altos, California.

Teenagers who feel that adult censorship of the Internet is an unnecessary infringement of their right to information have their own web page on the Internet entitled "Cyber Rights for Kids." While they acknowledge the need for these restrictions for young children, they encourage other teenagers to fight for the right to "pure information" on the Internet.

Emancipation and a Parent's Right to Consent. Parents have the right to grant or withhold their consent to most of their children's actions. Children have to comply with their parents' decisions unless the action is specifically allowed by the state (for example, applying for a driver's license), without a parental consent requirement (i.e., abortion laws), or if the child is fully or partially emancipated. Children are automatically emancipated when they reach the age of majority (18, 19, 20, or 21, depending on the state) or if they legally join the army or get married. Emancipation releases the parents from their duty to support the child and also gives the child more adult rights and responsibilities. A teenager who is financially independent may also become emancipated by mutual consent (parents and child) or by judicial decree. Although parents must give their explicit consent before a judge orders an emancipation, the courts could interpret parental refusal to support and shelter a child as an implied consent to emancipation.

In some instances a child may be partially emancipated from his or her parents for a specific purpose, by judicial decree (see Alicia Silverstone in Chapter 7), or automatically by state law. This situation arises frequently in the area of medical care where in some states children are allowed to receive medical treatment without parental consent.

Medical Care and Privacy Rights. The issue of a teenager's role in deciding his or her medical care is a thorny one. Parents have the authority to make decisions regarding medical care for their children, and states can intervene only if the decision places a child at risk. For instance, parents cannot prevent a child from receiving a lifesaving blood transfusion, even if it is against their religious beliefs.

A more interesting question is whether a child can refuse medical care in opposition to parents' wishes or a state mandate. Sixteen-year-old Billy Best ran away from his home in Massachusetts because he did not want to continue with his chemotherapy treatments, which made him nauseous and tired. His parents wanted him to continue with his treatments. Billy had the right to receive treatment for a life-threatening illness, but did he have the right to refuse it? (Adults do have this right.) "The reason I left," said Billy, "is because I could not stand going to the hospital every week. I feel like the medicine is killing me instead of helping me."[18]

Fifteen-year-old Benito Agrelo refused to undergo treatment to sustain a transplanted liver. He had been told that the transplanted liver would probably fail, even if he took his medicine, and, since the drugs had such painful side effects and "he couldn't play with any of his friends," he decided to let nature take its course and not continue with his treatment. The state, claiming to act in the boy's best interest, wanted to force Benny to take the treatment. It went to court to order him to be removed from his parents' home and admitted to the hospital. Judge Arthur Birkin met with Benny and his parents in the hospital and decided that Benny could go home. "I am tired of feeling the pain," said Benny. "I should have the right to make my own decision. I know the consequences, I know the problems."[19] Benny added that he had not given up the fight, just changed his idea of victory. He died two months later in his home.

To force a child to undergo painful and sometimes futile treatments becomes more difficult when the child is older and more independent. To avoid the trauma of involving an outside party (the court) to make a diffi-

This photo of Billy Best, taken in 1992, was used as a handout by police in their effort to try to locate him.

cult health-care decision for the child, some legal experts recommend partial emancipation under state law for minors who are above a specific age and who have been diagnosed with specific illnesses. They believe that this may be the safest and most objective way to empower older children to make independent decisions regarding their medical treatment.

Dr. Arthur Elter of the American Medical Association's adolescent health department raises the issue of empowering teenagers to care for their health when he feels that "most have not acquired the judgment that comes with adult experience."[20] He does encourage involving teenagers in the decision-making process. Dr. Arthur Caplan, director of bioethics at the University of Pennsylvania, thinks that teenagers have the right to refuse treatment if it can be determined on a case-by-case basis that the teenager is competent, has had experience with the treatment, and is making an informed decision. But he adds, "Acceptance of their refusal does not mean you stop trying to persuade them to receive the treatment."[21]

Commitment to Mental Institutions. The issue of medical treatment for minors also involves the area of mental health. In 1979 the Supreme Court ruled that minors were not entitled to the same precommitment procedural safeguards as adults. The Court's decision was based on the reasoning that a parent can usually be relied on to make this decision in the minor's best interests. (*Parham* v. *J.R.* 442 U.S. 584). The Court did require that before a child is "voluntarily admitted" into a mental institution by his parents, a staff physician must make an independent decision that the child is in need of this care. The Court also ruled that a neutral fact-finder must inquire into the child's background before voluntary admission. (This procedure is categorized as a "voluntary admission" since the decision is made voluntarily by the parents). The Court added another safeguard: Periodic evaluations of the minor are required to determine the need for continued commitment.

An earlier ruling by the Supreme Court established the right of sixteen-year-olds who have been voluntarily admitted into mental institutions to enter or leave these facilities over the objections of their parents. (*Bartley* v. *Kremens* 424 U.S. 964, 1976). Although the minor is not protected under the Constitution in this matter, state laws may offer more protective procedures. Some states, such as Virginia, require judicial review of this commitment if the minor objects.

In some states defiant minors may be admitted by their parents into locked psychiatric wards in private hospitals without precommitment hearings. The ability of adults to use this system to control disobedient and rebellious minors is a reality in some states. Described as a "hidden system of juvenile control," the Children's Defense Fund study found that nationwide at least 40 percent of these admissions of minors were inappropriate.[22]

The Abortion Controversy. The issue of abortion is a sensitive one, and even more so when it involves minors. In 1973, in *Roe* v. *Wade*, the Supreme Court overturned a Texas law making abortion a crime, on the grounds that a woman's right to privacy includes her decision to terminate a pregnancy. The country is split, though, on whether abortions should be legal or not. In the case of minors, states have passed laws to restrict free exercise of this right. In 1976 the Supreme Court ruled that a Missouri law that prohibited a doctor from performing an abortion on a minor without parental consent was unconstitutional (*Planned Parenthood* v. *Danforth* 428 U.S. 52). The Court stated that a parent's interest to terminate the pregnancy was not any more important than the privacy right of the "competent minor mature enough to have become pregnant." However, in later decisions the Court upheld one state statute that required the doctor to notify a parent before the abortion is performed and another statute that required the consent of a parent or judge. However, as a protection to the minor, the Court created the judicial bypass provision, allowing a minor to seek permission for an abortion from a judge instead of a parent who will then determine if she is mature enough to make the decision to have the abortion or not. Even if the court determines the minor is not mature enough to make the decision for herself, the judge can order the abortion if it is in the minor's best interest. Despite these rulings, many states, including New York, do not require parental consent or notification before a minor obtains an abortion. Opponents of mandatory parental involvement (notification or consent) argue that this requirement will result in teens delaying and avoiding timely medical help, which may cause more unwanted children and late-term abortions.

Dr. Renee Jenkins, chairman of Pediatrics and Child Health at Howard University, states that "we've found that when you involve the family it's a positive situation, but you can't force it. It won't work."[23] Dr. Luella Klein, an obstetrician and professor at Emory University, says that "parents always want to know what is going on with their children. But ask a teen what they want in health care and they say confidentiality."[24]

In a drastic effort to prevent teen pregnancies, prosecutors in Emmett, Idaho, are charging unmarried, pregnant teenagers and their boyfriends with violating a 1921 law banning fornication (sex between unmarried people). Most teenagers plead guilty and are placed on probation for three years. During this time they are required to complete high school, stay off alcohol, drugs, and cigarettes, and attend parenting classes. Although one Idaho teenager was unsuccessful in her attempt to challenge the narrow application of the law, the executive director of the Idaho ACLU agreed that targeting teenagers was a violation of their right to equal protection under the law.

On the international scene, abortion is banned by constitutional law in Ireland. In 1991 a fourteen-year-old girl was raped and became pregnant. Her parents attempted to take her to England, where abortions are legal, but the High Court in Dublin issued an injunction (a court order to stop the action) restraining the girl from leaving Ireland for the purposes of an abortion. The parents and young girl complied, but challenged this ruling in court. After much debate, the Irish Supreme Court lifted the travel restriction and the girl was able to secure the abortion.

Contraceptives. Related to the abortion issue is the question of birth control and minors. The ease with which minors can buy contraceptives varies from state to state. More than half the states allow teenagers to purchase prescription contraceptives (the pill, a diaphragm) after being informed of the risks, without parental consent.

More than half the states also permit minors to receive prenatal care and delivery services without parental consent or notification. All states except North Carolina allow minors to receive medical diagnosis and treatment for sexually transmitted diseases such as syphilis, gonorrhea, and herpes. Eleven states allow minors to give their own consent for HIV testing and treatment. And almost all the states and Washington, D.C., authorize confidential medical care and counseling for alcohol and other drug abuse. Despite the laws, when it comes to paying the doctor bills, unless it is a government-sponsored program, a parent's or guardian's participation is often needed.

Search and Seizure. Privacy rights also include the right to be free from intrusive searches, of either person or property, by the police or other government officials. Private citizens, including children, can be searched only by law-enforcement officials if there is probable cause to believe that the person is breaking the law. A court-issued search warrant, describing the person, place, and/or subjects of the search, and based on probable cause is necessary before a search may be started in one's home or place of business. A police officer can also frisk, or pat down, anyone suspected of carrying a weapon. Children who are apprehended do not have to answer any questions by the police or other officials, including school officials, other than to give their name and address, and they have the right to contact a parent or guardian. If minors are unreasonably frisked or searched, they should cooperate, but they should state loud and clear their objection to the search.

As in other areas of the law, the guidelines involving searchers become blurred when applied to children. Under the Exclusionary Rule, in effect since 1914, the re-sults of an illegal search are not allowed as evidence in court. Minors can invoke the exclusionary rule to pro-hibit evidence implicating them in criminal activity when it can be shown that their privacy rights were violated. Parents, however, can give police the right to lift this ban, by giving consent for a child's room, or book bag, or person to be searched.

Likewise, school officials, acting in place of the par-ents, can allow locker searches if there is a strong enough suspicion that the lockers are being used to hide illegal substances or weapons.

Privacy in School. School officials, acting *in loco parentis*, also have the right to search bags and purses. In *New Jersey* v. *T.L.O.* two high school students were caught smoking in the lavatory. One admitted to the offense and was suspended for three days. The other, a four-teen-year-old girl, denied the charge. The principal looked in her purse and found a pack of cigarettes. Look-ing deeper, he found rolling papers and, emptying her purse, he discovered a bag of marijuana and evidence of marijuana sales. Her parents were called and, in their presence, she was read her Miranda warnings ("You have the right to an attorney..."). After admitting to selling the drug, the girl was suspended for ten days.

The case then reached juvenile court, where she was charged with delinquency based on possession of mari-juana with intent to sell. The attorney hired by her par-ents challenged both the school suspension and the delinquency charge on the grounds that her Fourth Amendment rights—the right to a legal search—were violated. In deciding the case, the Supreme Court rec-ognized a child's right to a legitimate expectation of pri-

These students at Martin Luther King, Jr., High School in New York City pass through a metal detector each morning in an attempt by school and city officials to keep the school weapon-free.

vacy and agreed that the Fourth Amendment does not apply to searches by school officials. However, since the interest of school officials in maintaining discipline and order in schools outweighs the privacy interest of the student, a lesser standard for searches was justified. Under this test the Court ruled that the school officials in this case were within their bounds to search her purse. In defining this further, the Court said the search must be "reasonable under all of the circumstances" and cannot be excessively intrusive. The Court found the search both lawful and reasonable.

This standard is open to interpretation by courts around the country, and it is being applied in a variety of situations, with varying results. School officials in Colorado searched the car of a junior high school student parked on school grounds. The search was based on information that he drove another student suspected of selling drugs to school every morning. A duffel bag containing marijuana was found in the car, and he was charged with delinquency. The Court ruled that the search was reasonable. (In Re P.E.A., 754 P.2d 382 Colo., 1988). A New York State Appeals Court found that a fifteen-year-old student should not have been suspended for carrying a loaded weapon to school because the gun was found as a result of an unlawful search. A family court judge decided that it was not reasonable for the security guard to suspect that the handle of a gun was pulling down the pocket of the boy's leather jacket and excluded the gun from evidence.

Strip searches, which involve the visual inspection of a person's body, are far more intrusive. Reasonableness is a standard to determine if the search was necessary and whether it was conducted appropriately. These searches should be carried out in private, by a member of the same sex as the minor, when there is good reason to believe that the minor is in criminal possession of drugs or a weapon. A fifteen-year-old student was taken to the principal's office after she was found in the parking lot during school hours. A search of her purse revealed school "readmittance slips," which she should not have had in her possession. After being asked to empty her jeans pockets, she was then told to remove her jeans and bend over so the contents of her brassiere could be examined visually. The Court found that the search was unreasonable because school officials had no reasonable cause to suspect that the student was in possession of drugs. According to this ruling, school officials would have to prove a student's actions create a reasonable suspicion that a specific law has been broken and that it is reasonable to expect that a search would reveal evidence of this violation (*Cales* v. *Howell Public Schools* 635 F. Supp. 454 E.D. Mich., 1985). In another case the Court found that a school social worker should not have made a fourteen-year-old boy remove his clothes and pull his underwear out in front and back to search for $100 he was accused of stealing. The money was found in his underwear but was not allowed into evidence against him in a criminal proceeding because the search was too intrusive. The Court decided that although stealing is not to be condoned, it does not present the threat of immediate danger to others, which may warrant a strip search (*State* v. *Mark Anthony B.* 433 S.E.2d 41 W.Va., 1993).

What about across-the-board searches that are not based on individualized suspicion? James Acton, age twelve, from a small logging town in Oregon, wanted to play football but refused to submit to a mandatory drug test because he felt that the school had no reason to think that he was taking drugs. The test, a urine sample collected in school (in private), was school-board policy, to combat a growing drug problem, especially among the athletes. Following James's lead, his parents refused to consent to the drug test and challenged the blanket testing program for violating James's Fourth Amendment rights. James lost. Justice Antonin Scalia, writing for the Court, ruled that students have a lesser Fourth Amendment right than adults, especially because of the growing drug problem. Athletes, he said, have an even lesser expectation of privacy considering that they are routinely expected to take showers and also that they have a somewhat exalted "role model" position in schools. "School sports are not for the bashful," he said.[25] Justice Sandra Day O'Connor disagreed, writing for the dissent that this policy of blanket drug testing was excessively intrusive, particularly destructive of privacy, and offensive to personal dignity. She concluded that it would have been "far more reasonable" to limit the test to those students with disciplinary problems (*Veronia School District* v. *Acton*, 1995). The Court did not answer the question whether random testing of all students would be constitutional. To date, Court rulings have generally established that blanket searches of lockers, school desks, and use of metal detectors are reasonable in light of their deterrent effect on drug use and violence. David Rubin, a school attorney from New Jersey and an expert in the field of education law, comments: "It may be easier to board an El Al [Israeli national airline] flight than to pass through today's schoolhouse gate." But he adds that once students are "within the custody and control of school officials, students still enjoy basic constitutional liberties, though tailored to fit the unique circumstances of the public school setting."[26]

Throughout this chapter, we have seen how an individual's right to privacy is balanced with other rights such as a parent's right to consent or the public's right to know. We have also seen how courts examine government policies in light of their impact on an individual's civil liberties. In each instance, the court must determine which right is superior or which one takes precedence over the other.

The privacy rights of minors are usually entrusted to their parents, in the belief that an adult will, with care and experience, guide the child's growth into maturity and protect him or her from exploitation and exposure to drugs, violence, and pornography. When a parent does not do this, there are occasions where the state will step in. Adolescents and teenagers have a better chance of protecting their privacy by exercising their freedoms responsibly and discussing these issues openly with their parents or guardians in the home. In public, the key to preserving privacy rights is knowledge. Learn the laws and speak up if you think your rights are being violated!

CHAPTER SIX

DISCRIMINATION

I want to be remembered as a person who stood up to injustice, who wanted a better world for young people, and most of all...as a person who wanted to be free.[1]

Rosa Parks

Claudette Colvin, age fifteen, boarded a public bus in Montgomery, Alabama. The year was 1955. Signs at the back of the bus said "coloreds"; the front seats were reserved for "whites only." This was the law since 1900, the year that Montgomery became the first city to run an electric trolley system. Claudette walked to a seat in the middle of the bus. These seats could be used by blacks only if whites didn't want them. The bus crossed into the white section of Montgomery. White high school students boarded, at first staring, then complaining that Claudette was breaking the law. The driver stopped the bus and ordered Claudette to move. She refused. A policeman was called to the bus. He stood over Claudette and demanded she move. And she refused again, even when two more policemen stepped onto the bus. "No, I do not have to get up. It's my constitutional right to sit here as much as that lady."[2] The policemen knocked Claudette's books down and dragged her off the bus and arrested her.

When asked later why she did not sit that day in the "coloreds" seating, Claudette answered that she had been inspired by her history lessons in school. "I knew I had to do something," she said. "I just didn't know where or when."[3] She remembered reading about King John of England who, in 1215, was forced by his subjects to sign the Magna Carta, a charter of civil liberties that curtailed the absolute power of the English kings. She also could not forget the words of the American Revolution fighter Patrick Henry, "Give me liberty or give me death." She had read, and drew strength from, the Constitution, a document that promised equal protection to all citizens. This was her legacy, too.

Although it took more than a hundred years to accomplish, the Fourteenth Amendment, ratified in 1868, is now an established law. No American citizen, including a child, can be singled out for special treatment, either favorably or unfavorably, on the basis of sex, race, religion, or national origin. This is reinforced by federal civil rights laws. Any state or municipal law or policy that affects the public must not contradict the federal regulation.

History. In 1863, President Abraham Lincoln signed the Emancipation Proclamation, which declared all slaves forever free. Two years later, the South surrendered to the North, and Reconstruction, designed to help the seceded states with their reentry into the Union, began. The transition, however, did not go smoothly. The South continued to resist the concept that "Negroes" (the term given to people of African origin) were free to enjoy the rights of every American citizen. Black codes were passed in the South barring blacks from voting, from schools and juries, from owning weapons, from holding meetings without white people present, and from walking on the streets after dark.

In rapid succession, the Thirteenth, Fourteenth, and Fifteenth amendments were passed. Slavery was abolished by the Thirteenth Amendment, in 1865, and it was backed by the Civil Rights Act of 1866, which required states to respect the civil rights of all citizens, irrespective of race or color. The Fourteenth Amendment, in 1868, provided that all persons born in the United States, or those who have become citizens, have full citizenship rights. It also stated that "no state shall make or enforce any law which shall abridge the privileges or immunities of citizens of the United States; nor shall any state deprive any person of life, liberty, or property, without due process of law; nor deny to any person within its jurisdiction the equal protection of the laws." The Fifteenth Amendment, ratified in 1870, gave voting rights to all citizens regardless of race, creed, or color.

Despite these advances, some white leagues still wanted to exclude blacks from political and social integration. Written and unwritten laws, known as "Jim Crow" laws (such as requiring separate Bibles for black and white witnesses in court or for storing textbooks used by black students separately from those used by white students), fostered segregation. The Red Cross segregated Negro blood in blood banks until the 1940s. Signs saying "whites only" dotted the Southern landscape. Challenges to this treatment often led to beatings or lynchings. In addition, literacy tests and grandfather clauses (allowing a person to vote only if his grandfather voted) were loopholes that prevented the law on black voting from being upheld. Groups like the Ku Klux Klan were formed to prevent the execution of the new laws. Because of this resistance, and because often the law-enforcement officers looked the other way, the laws, in practice, offered little protection.

This continued resistance to equal rights was sanctioned in 1896 when a ruling from the U.S. Supreme Court in *Plessy* v. *Ferguson*[4] established the "separate but equal" standard. Plessy, a black man, challenged his eviction from a white railroad car, and the Court decided that blacks could be excluded if separate facilities were provided. This ruling stood until 1954 when the Supreme Court, in the case of *Brown* v. *Board of Education of Topeka, Kansas*, said that separating people on the basis of race always involves some form of inequality and denies to black children equal protection of the laws guaranteed by the Fourteenth Amendment of the Constitution.[5] Segregation in schools was made illegal. This was a milestone in children's rights, since the Supreme Court emphasized the importance of education and recognized the violation of a child's constitutional right by segregation. Despite this, segregation, sanctioned by practice, persisted in the South.

About the time that Claudette fought her private battle, a larger movement was being launched to fight discrimination in the South. Under the guidance of Martin Luther King, Jr., black and white Americans boycotted segregated buses, and "sit-ins" were staged in whites-only facilities. Many young people, from all over the country, joined the movement.

The issue was addressed in 1961 when the Supreme Court declared segregation illegal on buses (most bus companies dealt with interstate travel, which automatically put them under federal jurisdiction) and in bus station waiting rooms. Now Claudette and any other nonwhite person could sit undisturbed on any seat in the bus.

And in 1964, President Lyndon B. Johnson signed the Civil Rights Act into law. It was hailed as "the greatest single triumph for human rights in our country since the Emancipation Proclamation."[6] Along with the Voting Rights Act (1965) and the Fair Housing Act (1968), it made segregation illegal in hiring, voting, housing, and in public places including schools.

Civil Rights Today. Civil rights laws are still being utilized to check discriminatory practices and compensate victims of civil rights abuses. In a recent case (1995), Denny's, a national restaurant chain, was ordered to pay more than $54 million to black customers who were discriminated against in the restaurants. One of the plaintiffs, seventeen-year-old Kristina Ridgeway, told how she and a group of her friends were asked for a cover charge and prepayment of their meals. Their white classmates had no such restrictions. "I was very upset," said Kristina. "Both my parents are from the South and they had to grow up with this kind of thing, and they would always tell me that I wouldn't have to deal with stuff like this."[7] Denny's also agreed, through the National Association for the Advancement of Colored People (NAACP), to finance job programs and contracts for minorities at a cost of $1 billion.

In Union Point, Georgia, merchants agreed to pay $265,000 in damages to twelve young black residents whose names were put on a list of "troublemakers" and who were told that entering local shops could result in arrests for trespassing. As they had never been convicted for shoplifting, or any other crime, the youths claimed this violated their civil rights. According to one mother, winning the case was a vindication for the young victims, who, instead of running from the accusation, fought for their rights.[8]

Although the struggle to secure equal treatment in America was fought mainly by one race, it gave the right of equal treatment to all American citizens of any race, sex, or national origin.

Equal Protection in Schools. After *Brown* v. *Board of Education of Topeka, Kansas,* established that "separate but equal" schools violated the Fourteenth Amendment right to equal opportunity for black students, schools could no longer be segregated. How to desegregate, how to rectify the effects of past discrimination, were questions that led to years of volatile confrontations between blacks (and other ethnic groups) and whites and have led to complaints of "reverse discrimination." This issue is being raised by white students around the country who view "affirmative action" policies, designed to counteract past discrimination, as unfairly placing the burdens of the past on the present.

Boston, a city that favored the abolition of slavery yet resisted segregation through forced busing, is the seat of a new discrimination controversy a century later. Boston Latin is the oldest and one of the best public high schools in the city. Graduates include five signers of the Declaration of Independence, Ralph Waldo Emerson, and Leonard Bernstein. Twelve-year-old Julia McLaughlin applied for admission, but even though her scores qualified her to be admitted, she was denied a place because of a quota setting aside 35 percent of the places for black and Hispanic students. Her father challenged that nineteen-year-old policy, saying he was "not trying to roll back desegregation," but he just wanted his daughter to attend the school of her choice, and the one she deserved.[9] Julia sued in federal court, and the judge ordered that she should attend Boston Latin while the suit was being decided. Officials said the quota was necessary to prevent resegregation, and that diversity is beneficial to all students. Students have a variety of opinions. Talia Whyte, a black sophomore, called the policy of quotas stupid. "A lot of people are going to think I didn't earn my way," she states, adding, "of course, there is discrimination, there will always be discrimination."[10] Peter Black, a white senior, said, "It [diversity] makes the school more interesting."[11] Ellen King, a white junior, said, "To be told you are not going to get in because of your color is sickening."[12] Saamre Mekuria-Grillo, a black sophomore, saw both sides: "I don't think it's fair that people who score really high on a test don't get in because of their race, but I also don't think it is an even starting point with black and white people."[13] Saamre identified the main point of contention in reverse discrimination suits—there is not a level playing field in Boston or most other places in the country. Disadvantaged students often need catch-up work to prepare them for schools such as Boston Latin. In New York some schools are providing these students with special help in math and science.

In November 1996, the Boston School Committee decided to replace its racial quota system in Boston Latin and two other top public schools with a new policy that would still "insure that students in Boston from every racial and ethnic group will have equal access"[14] to these schools. Judge J. Arthur Garrity, who imposed the quota system in 1976, heard Julia's case twenty years later. He says he has changed his mind and views the quota system as "constitutionally suspect."[15]

In 1978 the Supreme Court wrestled with the issue of quotas for colleges in *U.S. v. Bakke*. Twice rejected from medical school, Alan Bakke sued on the basis that minority candidates with lower scores were admitted because of an affirmative-action quota that set aside 16 out of 100 places for students of racial minorities. Rather than stating that any form of preference is invalid, the Court specified that the quota system violated Bakke's rights under the Fourteenth Amendment, and the Civil Rights Act, which forbids exclusion in a federally funded school on the basis of race. Although the ruling prohibited quotas, it did not invalidate admission policies that promote a diverse student population.

Some people view this ruling as a legal setback for minorities. They believe that it is a reversal from the commitment to eliminate the "badges of slavery" (results of oppression). Others interpret it as a step toward judging a person only on the basis of achievement rather than race. "There is a good reason to think that we are looking toward the end of most racial preferences," said Stephen L. Carter, author of *Reflections of an Affirmative Action Baby*. These preferences have long been justified as "transitional," he said, and when they come to an end it will not be a disaster but a "challenge and a chance."[16]

Gender Discrimination. Discrimination is not limited to race. Susan B. Anthony, a leader in the Women's Rights Movement, drafted a proposal to amend the Constitution to give women the right to vote, and forty years later, in 1918, women were given that right. It took two more years to ratify the Nineteenth Amendment. Even then, until 1928 women had to be thirty years of age and older to vote. The voting age was lowered to age eighteen for all citizens in 1971.

The rights of women have traditionally been considered incidental to the rights of men. Over the years, women have challenged all-male institutions in America, in particular those that are dedicated to defense. Since 1976, West Point Academy has included women in its military service program, and in 1995, Rebecca Morier graduated first in her class of 988 cadets. Both the Air Force Academy and the Naval Academy have also accepted women since 1976, one year after an Act of Congress required service academies to admit women.

When Shannon Faulkner, a high school honors graduate with a varsity athletic record, decided to apply to the Citadel, a military academy in South Carolina that had been all male for 152 years, she did not indicate her sex on the application. The Citadel admitted her and then revoked her admission when they discovered she was a woman. Faulkner sued the academy and was joined in her action by the Justice Department and the ACLU. Also on her side was a federal district court ruling that allowed her to attend classes as a day student until the case was heard. Against her was the resolution of the South Carolina legislature supporting single-gender education. It offered the Justice Department a proposal to counter Faulkner's suit, stating that a leadership

Shannon Faulkner is escorted to the barracks on her first day as a member of the Citadel corps of cadets.

program would be provided for women at Converse College, a private women's college in South Carolina. According to Marcia Greenberger, co-president of the National Women's Law Center in Washington, this alternative provided "a separate and unequal situation" since it lacked the benefits of an alumni network, support systems, and the prestigious reputation associated with the Citadel.[17]

After two years and a million dollars in legal fees, an appeals court ruled that Faulkner could attend the Citadel as a full-time cadet. The court admonished the Citadel for spending public money to defend an admissions policy that denied women their rights guaranteed by the equal protection clause of the Constitution. On learning of her victory Faulkner said, "It's not just for women. It's for everyone. If you believe in something, go for it."[18] Faulkner gained entry to an all-male military institution, but due to harassment (some of her classmates wore T-shirts saying "1,952 Bulldogs and one Bitch") and physical distress suffered during "hell week," when cadets are subjected to intense physical and mental endurance tests, Faulkner left the Citadel after less than a week. She was escorted off campus by federal marshals because of death threats to her and her family. Despite this outcome, Valerie Vodjik, Faulkner's attorney, warned, "If the Citadel thinks it can solve the problem through Shannon's leaving, they're dead wrong."[19]

Her prediction came true in June 1996 when the Supreme Court ruled that Virginia Military Institute, a state-supported military college, violated the equal-protection clause of the Constitution by excluding women. Chief Justice William Rehnquist also invalidated the remedy of sending women to a state-supported "leadership program" in a nearby women's college. Four women were admitted into the Citadel in the fall of 1996 in compliance with the Supreme Court ruling.

Men, too, have had reason to bring discrimination suits against institutions. An all-girls public school that recently opened in Harlem, in New York City is being challenged by the New York Civil Liberties Union and the New York Civil Rights Coalition for being discriminatory to boys. The school was conceived on the premise that girls in poor neighborhoods fare better in classrooms without boys. Although the NYCLU believes that the school should recruit boys, a *New York Times* report revealed that boys did not show much interest in applying to similar schools in other states when the single-sex policy was changed.

Rights of the Disabled. Benjamin Bolger was diagnosed with dyslexia when he was a preschooler. Instead of recognizing Benjamin's special needs, his teachers insisted that he would eventually catch up with the other kids. Inevitably nothing changed, and Benjamin was called stupid and slow. Rather than pursue his remedies in court, his mother dedicated her time to reading to him and teaching him at home. At the age of thirteen, Benjamin was admitted to the University of Michigan. He graduated first in his class of more than 4,000 with a 4.0 grade-point average. He is now a student at Yale Law School, and at age twenty is an advocate for the disabled and dyslexic.

Benjamin Bolger's dream as a child was to be a great architect like Frank Lloyd Wright. However, his personal experiences have changed his course "not to create the ideal building but the ideal society,"[20] sensitive to the needs of all people.

Not all stories of disabled students are as exceptional as Benjamin's. Not every mother can dedicate all her time to one child, nor will every home-schooled child become so successful. Yet the opportunity to bring out the special qualities and talents of every child may be a reality if the child's needs are recognized and addressed. Since the 1975 Individuals with Disabilities Education Act (IDEA), a federal law guarantees a free public school education to all children with any disability from birth to age twenty-one. The act requires states to provide accommodations for appropriate instruction to the disabled child in neighborhood schools. The Department of Education reported that more than 5 million children with disabilities attended regular schools during 1994.[21] The largest group was those with learning disabilities, followed by speech-language disorders, learning disabled, emotionally disabled, hard of hearing, visually impaired, and health impaired.

Section 504 of the Rehabilitation Act of 1973 became the operative law in 1977 to prohibit discrimination against disabled students who qualified for admission to college. They are entitled to special counseling and instructional aids like sign-language interpreters and textbooks in Braille. One in every nine undergraduates has a disability, according to the American Council on Education.[22] The number of disabled youths attending college has doubled in the past ten years.

Students With AIDS. The impact of AIDS (acquired immunodeficiency syndrome) has created unique and difficult situations involving discrimination and individual rights. "This issue pits the rights of those with the disease to attend school, against the fears of other children and their parents."[23]

Ryan White, an honor student from Kokomo, Indiana, was thirteen years old when he was diagnosed with AIDS. He contracted this fatal disease from injections he received to control his hemophilia. The administrator at the school he attended asked him to leave, his classmates taunted him and trashed his locker, his mother's car tires were slashed, and a bullet was fired into his home, yet his parents went to court and won the right to readmit him to school.

"It was really my decision [to go to court]," he said in an interview on the Phil Donahue television talk show. "I was bored out of my mind sitting at home all the time. It was great the first couple of weeks. You're out of school, no homework, no nothing. But then it got to the point where you were looking at the ceiling the whole time."[24] When Ryan returned to school he still met with hostility from parents and was ignored by children who were not allowed to play with him. Finally, his family decided to move to another town that was more accepting of Ryan and his family. Ryan died shortly after his television debut after battling AIDS for nearly six years. His courage was an inspiration to the whole world, but he said he was just "trying to be like everyone else," testing himself "to find out how much I can take."

AIDS is a fatal disease that is known to be transmitted from one person to another only through the exchange of body fluids (blood or semen). The Centers for Disease Control (CDC) and most medical experts state that AIDS cannot be transmitted through casual

After winning a court battle to be allowed to return to school, Ryan White waits for the school bus near his home in Indiana.

contact. This means that contact in a school setting does not pose a significant risk for infection. Unless a child has an advanced case of AIDS, he or she should not be excluded from the classroom.

People who have been diagnosed with AIDS are protected under the Americans With Disabilities Act, yet parents of children with AIDS meet with resistance from school boards and parents of other students when they attempt to enroll their kids in public schools. School districts either exclude the students with AIDS, responding if the student takes the matter to court, or they adopt policies that deal with each student individually. Recent damage awards against school districts that have refused admission to students with AIDS may stop this policy. The CDC has recommended that each school district should evaluate each case individually. A program can then be structured for the infected child based on recommendations by an expert panel. This group can consist of the child's parent or guardian, public health personnel, school officials, and the child's physician. In Florida, a judge structured a ruling that addressed the rights of all parties involved.

Influencing Supreme Court Decisions. The dramatic swing from the ruling in *Plessy* v. *Ferguson* (establishing "separate but equal" standards) to *Brown* v. *Board of Education* (reversing the "separate but equal" ruling), illustrates how social, political, and economic changes in America can and do influence Supreme Court interpretations of the Fourteenth Amendment. As Talia Whyte, from Boston Latin, said, "There will always be discrimination."

The important lesson to be learned is that the equal protection clause guarantees every American citizen, including children, the right to challenge any policy that violates this right. Once a legitimate grievance is identified, parents or guardians can be called upon to help with the legal process of filing petitions and conducting negotiations. And if this fails, the option of legal intervention, of taking it to court, exists, no matter how time consuming or expensive.

ON THE JOB: CHILD LABOR LAWS

Put the men to work and let the babies go home!
Oshkosh, Wisconsin, 1893

Tommy McCoy was fourteen when he landed his dream job—bat boy for the Savannah Cardinals' farm team. He earned ten dollars per game, but he was not in it for the money or the fame or prestige. He was bat boy because he loved baseball—the smells, sights, cheers, the winning and even the losing. He was an important part of America's favorite sport, and he was not alone. Bat boys have been hauling bats and shagging balls ever since the first games were played in the middle of the nineteenth century.

Tommy was fired, however, a few games into the 1994 season, when an investigator for Georgia's Labor Department's wage and hour division blew the whistle on the hours that Tommy worked. During the school year, fourteen- and fifteen-year-olds could not work more than three hours a day, eighteen hours a week, or after 7 P.M. These restrictions were relaxed during the summer. Forty-hour workweeks were allowed then, and minors could work until 9 P.M. But many baseball games last later than 9 P.M., so this still meant that bat boys and bat girls had to be sixteen or over.

Tommy's problem was written up in the newspapers and attracted the attention of Labor Secretary Robert B. Reich. He said the application of the law to Tommy looked "silly," and that Tommy's "health and well-being" were not adversely affected.[1] (The impairment of children's "health and well-being" was the major reason that child-labor laws were passed.) Reich gave Tommy a reprieve while the U.S. Labor Department studied the issue of minors working as bat boys and bat girls and their equivalents in all professional sports. One year later, the Clinton administration, in one of the first changes in child-labor hours since 1938, eliminated the restrictions on the number of hours that fourteen- and fifteen-year-olds can work as bat boys and bat girls, and as their equivalents in all professional sports. By this time, Tommy, who had been working provisionally during the year, was sixteen, and was no longer restricted, even by the old law.

"This worked for me because the media got ahold of it," said Tommy. "That got people involved, and it [the new regulation] is a lot better now."[2]

Special Treatment for Sports. Many children's-rights activist groups do not support eliminating restrictions on when minors can work, even though it affects very few teenagers. It was the Child Labor Coalition's "unassailable conclusion" that the change will cause other industries to ask for the relaxation of child-labor laws.[3] "What makes sports so special?" is the question that administrators at the Labor Department are waiting for. Why not longer hours at the amusement park? the restaurant? the grocery store?

Was this a common-sense approach to enforcing child-labor laws, or an erosion of hard-won child-labor regulations? The National Educational Association, the National Parent-Teacher Association, and the American Academy of Pediatrics are among the groups that believe the wrong message was being sent to the employment community when this new regulation was instituted. The Labor Department insists that because the decision was narrowly focused, it will not spread to other professions.

What Is Child Labor? Children have historically been exploited in the area of labor. Until the first part of the twentieth century, factory owners could, and did, actually work children to death. Some parents also were not above using their children for financial gain, even putting their children up for sale. Textile mills, especially exploitive of child labor, often used children while men went unemployed. This situation may have inspired the poem by the Quaker poet Sarah Cleghorn in her book *Portrait and Protest*:

> The golf links lie so near the mill
> That almost every day
> The laboring children can look out
> And see the men at play.[4]

This cartoon, from the February 27, 1913, issue of Life magazine, shows that the sentiment against child labor was by this time growing stronger and louder.

because parents still have the right to keep a child's paycheck, children are especially vulnerable to abuse. In response, the government has established laws designed to protect children's rights in the area of employment.

It is these laws and restrictions that define what child labor is. If federal and state restrictions differ, the stricter one rules. For example, federal laws restrict minors from operating elevators, working in coal mines, manufacturing bricks, or driving motor vehicles while on the job. The state of Illinois restricts minors even further, not allowing them to work in bowling alleys or privately owned skating rinks. It was not until 1941 that the Supreme Court upheld child-labor laws enacted by the Fair Labor Standards Act of 1938. This was the first indication in the area of labor that the courts recognized their role over the parental role in protecting children.

Laws enacted most recently in the state of Washington were designed to protect children's educational interests as well as their health and safety. This could be a welcome protection or an annoying restriction, but either way it illustrates how child-labor laws evolve.

Rules and Regulations. Every minor who wants to work must get a work permit. Most schools issue them. These permits help the state keep track of the minor's employment conditions. Every person who works, including minors, must also have a Social Security number. This can be obtained from the local Social Security office. Minors may or may not be paid the minimum wage (the lowest pay allowed by law) for certain jobs such as baby-sitting, or if they work part-time or are in training. A minor may be eligible for unemployment insurance if he or she loses a job. Usually states require one to have worked full-time for a certain number of weeks to be eligible for unemployment. Any specific work-related questions or complaints should be addressed to the state Department of Labor.

Exploitation. Some individuals say that children are still being robbed of their health, their youth, and their lives by workplace hazards. Statistics back this up. In 1993 the National Safe Workplace Institute estimated there were 59,000 children per federal child-labor-law investigator.[5] This makes it impossible for every violation to be detected. Spot checks of commercial onion fields in Texas revealed hundreds of violators of child labor during the 1993 spring harvest.[6] In California in 1994, federal and state inspectors found employers in the garment industry who locked fire doors and worked thirteen-year-old children for nine hours at a stretch.[7] In June 1995, six workers in America under the age of eighteen were killed on the job.[8] According to the Department of Labor's Bureau of Labor Statistics, sixty-seven minors in America under the age of eighteen were killed on the job in 1994.[9]

Even the Girl Scouts are under fire. Some parents, troop leaders, and even the scouts themselves are questioning whether selling cookies is a form of exploitation, as the girls receive very little of the profit. Most of the money goes to support the Girl Scout's huge bureaucracy. More than half of the $357 million spent a year by the scouts for their management comes from cookie sales. The troops get 10 percent of the money collected. "There's incredible pressure on these little girls to sell," one attorney said. "The scouts are used as unpaid salespeople."[10]

To Work or to Play. Since child-labor laws were first passed in the 1930s, there has been constant redefinition of how these laws are carried out. Before 1938, parents or guardians had the sole decision-making power over how much and where their children worked. The passage of these laws let in a wedge of power from the government that has been striking deeper and deeper into this parental authority. And now the child is in the picture, asking for further rights.

These rights, however, are not always consistently for or against longer hours or safer conditions. The broad umbrella of child-labor laws, some say, can infringe on a personal liberty such as the right to work, or it can protect against a child being taken advantage of or put in a dangerous situation.

A case that demonstrates how child-labor laws can infringe on what some feel is a personal liberty is the Shiloh True Light Church of Christ case, now before the Supreme Court. The Shiloh True Light Church of Christ, acting as both parents and a church, say they have the right to raise their children according to their beliefs. This means allowing children as young as eight to drive forklifts and work long hours at a masonry company owned by church members. The Labor Department charged the firm with violating child-labor laws because children under eighteen were performing hazardous jobs.

The case has been in the courts since 1986, and until it is resolved, children under sixteen cannot work. "If you let a child wait that long, they don't want to work," said a church member. "Some of these kids can come out and build a whole house for themselves, and it makes them real happy. Now they are miserable."[11] The church feels that work is virtuous, that it provides vocational training for its children, and that the children benefit by sharing a trust account worth almost half a million dollars. Does the government have a right to intervene?

Further Examples of Restrictions. In Lansing, Michigan, the Labor Department used a three-day sting operation to uncover violators at six Michigan restaurants, including the Old County Buffet Restaurant.[12] Fourteen- and fifteen-year-olds were working more hours, or later hours, than legally allowed during the school week, and fourteen- to seventeen-year-olds were operating hazardous equipment, such as meat slicers. Managers of the restaurant pleaded that they were unaware that federal and state regulations differed and that they must adhere to the strictest regulation. The restaurant administration staff said the kids employed were saving for college and had permission slips from their parents, asking for jobs for their children. The restaurant said it would no longer hire kids under fifteen, or let minors work past 7 P.M.

Washington State went one step further. Amber Slane worked at the McDonald's in Rinton, Washington.[13] By the time she was fifteen, she had $2,000 saved for college. Her employee paid Amber and other teenage employees their hourly wage to complete their homework before and after their shifts. He also gave cash bonuses for good grades. He liked the energy and enthusiasm that teenagers brought to the job, and they responded by doing well both in school and at work.

But a three-year study by a Washington State labor committee, also endorsed by the Washington State Pediatric Association, concluded that students who work more than 20 hours per week during the school year risk failing even the most basic levels of English, math, and reading. As a result, in 1992, Washington adopted regulations that created the nation's strictest child-labor laws. Minors sixteen and seventeen had their workweek cut in half, to twenty hours, and fourteen- and fifteen-year-olds went from eighteen to fifteen hours a week. The type of work permitted was limited, too. Teenagers could no longer work at windowsills, on scaffolds, or in freezers and meat coolers.[14] If a child was permanently injured, or killed, on the job, the employer could be charged with a Class C felony with a prison term of up to five years. Does this mean that teenagers cannot work at a drive-up window, employers asked? Or, if a teenager was getting french fries from the freezer and slipped, could the employer be sent to jail?

Washington was the first state in the nation to restrict minors' working conditions and hours based on health, safety, and education. With this law, the state is widening its protective net beyond the classroom and into the home where parents are usually ultimately in control.

Child-Labor Law Protections. These same child-labor laws can work in a positive way to protect children in situations that are truly dangerous. They can also prevent exploitation by a management that might try to disregard them. When it is perceived that a child is working too many hours or in a dangerous situation, the protective umbrella of child-labor laws form a structure defining how children are supposed to be treated. The laws give minors the option to challenge the management and enforce the law in their favor through the Labor Department.

In just such a case, teenagers working for Food Lion, Inc., a fast-growing supermarket chain, won $16.2 million, the largest settlement ever by a private employer over a wage-and-hour violation. The complaint against Food Lion was brought by the Labor Department after an eighteen-month investigation, which revealed "widespread and extensive" violations, such as some teenagers operating dangerous machinery and being asked to work "off the clock" (overtime and without pay). By settling out of court, Food Lion did not admit to the violations, avoided years of litigation, and invested their dollars "in our workforce," according to Food Lion President Tom E. Smith.[15] The law that the Shiloh True Light Church of Christ is challenging is the same one that protected the teenagers who were working in the Food Lion grocery stores.

In a related case, in 1993, the Great Atlantic and Pacific Tea Company (A&P) agreed to pay almost half a million dollars to settle more than 900 federal child-labor law violations. The Labor Department charged the A&P with illegally employing minors, most of whom probably knew they were not working within the guidelines of the child-labor laws. But even if the minor is aware of the violation, it is the employer's responsibility for knowing and following the law, and it is the employer, not the minor, who will be punished if the laws are broken.

In 1994 the Labor Department raised the penalties for safety violations that result in a serious injury to a minor. The penalty runs from $10,000 per injury to $100,000 per violation. Employers are looking at a possibly hefty sum to be paid, since each injury usually involves more than one violation.

Volunteer Work or Slavery. The reverse side of working for wages is working for none, or volunteering. Under child-labor regulations, the state can stipulate that minors may volunteer their services for a variety of causes. Some schools have implemented this. Volunteer work is a requirement for graduation from Liberty High School in Bethlehem, Pennsylvania. Teenager Lynn Steirer sued the school district, comparing the requirement to slavery and, therefore, in violation of her constitutional rights. Although Lynn volunteers fifteen hours a week, she said, "I don't believe it is right to force someone to do community service....if they made it an elective course, it would be fine."[16] The Supreme Court did not agree. Lynn's claim was denied.

This same rule over mandatory volunteer work is being challenged in New York. Parents are claiming that the government once again is overstepping its bounds and interfering with their right as parents to raise their children without state interference. And in Maryland a bill was introduced in the state legislature making voluntary community service a requirement for graduation from all schools in the state. This is now Maryland law. Will it be a role model for other states?

Emancipation. If minors are legally emancipated, they can work long and odd hours at a profession of their choice in order to support themselves. Along with losing their right to control, parents are also released from their duty to support. Actress Alicia Silverstone became emancipated at age fifteen, while working on the movie *The Crush.* Her agent told her and her parents that she needed to be emancipated to work the hours the movie required. Ms. Silverstone wanted the part, so she stood before the judge and told him she was living on her own and supporting herself. She was granted emancipation.

Whose Money Is It? While it is the parents' duty to support their children, parents are given the right to keep and use any income their children might earn. However, this general rule is modified by state laws that allow children to keep their earnings unless parents give the employer notice to the contrary. How does this affect young movie stars or child athletes who enter into contracts worth millions? Along with parental consent needed to enter into these contracts, state laws also require court supervision of the terms in order to prevent exploitation of the child. Wages are held in special funds until the child reaches the age of majority. Despite these precautions, problems still can arise. Kit Culkin, the actor Macaulay Culkin's father and manager, is paid 7.5 percent of Macaulay's earnings, which are thought to be about $50 million. Because Macaulay works and earns a great deal of money, his family lives with a certain amount of comfort. Yet, according to his mother, Macaulay hired his father and can, therefore, fire him. The situation is compounded by a custody battle between Macaulay's parents, which puts management of his money at issue. This upside-down version of family life is an indicator of what can happen when children earn large sums of money.

Keeping Up With the Times. Children's-rights activists started lobbying for child-labor laws early in the twentieth century when children had to be protected not only from employers but also from their parents. In 1916 and 1918 child-labor legislation passed by Congress was overturned by the Supreme Court. It wasn't until 1941 that a federal law against child labor was upheld. Although this was a huge step toward the curbing of abuse in the workplace, the legislation was largely protective in nature. Child-labor laws continue to be based more on what the state perceives is for the good of the child. The process of defining and procuring the rights for what children might want has been slower. Federal and state governments want to maintain their superior status of protection, but in some instances what the government might see as protection, children and parents may see as infringement of rights. As a result, more and more laws are being challenged.

CHAPTER EIGHT

CRIMES AND PUNISHMENT

"No, no," said the Queen. "Sentence first—verdict afterwards."

"Stuff and nonsense!" said Alice loudly. "The idea of having the sentence first."

"Hold your tongue!" said the Queen, turning purple.

"I won't!" said Alice.

"Off with her head!" the Queen shouted at the top of her voice.

Alice's Adventures in Wonderland
and *Through the Looking Glass*
by Lewis Carroll

David, seventeen, charged with first-degree felony, explosive device found in school locker, bomb threats, eight schools closed, possible seven years in jail.

Eric, fourteen, convicted of second-degree murder, choked and crushed the head of a four-year-old boy, sentenced to nine years in prison, the first four to be served in a juvenile detention facility.

Jacob, ten, and Damien, fourteen, convicted of second-degree murder, shot female victim in the head for $80, sentenced to state custody until age twenty-one. "It was a game. It wasn't to kill the lady. It wasn't supposed to be like that."

These four minors were too young to vote, legally drink, or work unrestricted hours at any job of their choosing, and three of the four were even too young to drive. But although these boys did not enjoy the privileges given to adults, they were held to the same standard of responsibility as adults when they stopped acting like children and committed "adult crimes." For these crimes, three of the four received adult sentences.

Records of the Federal Bureau of Investigation (FBI) show that in 1994 there were 527 arrests for violent crime per 100,000 youths aged ten to seventeen.[1] As in other areas of the law where minors are given more responsibility for their actions and for determining the course of their lives, juveniles who commit serious, violent crimes are held responsible for the consequences as if they were adults. Three quarters of those adults questioned in a *USA Today*/CNN Gallup Poll agree. The message seems to be "if you're old enough to do the crime, you are old enough to do the time."

This is a reversal to the time when children were tried in adult courts and given long sentences in adult prisons for violent and nonviolent crimes. It stems from a public consensus that juvenile courts are not the most appropriate forum for violent criminals, even if those criminals are juveniles. Society is fighting back against increasing violence by treating minors as adults when they commit a serious crime, such as murder, rape, kidnapping, arson, and carjacking. Instead of handing down a lenient sentence in hopes of reforming the child, or tempering the ruling because of the youth's background, nationwide legislation is reflecting a trend to protect the public by treating the child who commits a violent adult crime as an adult.

Many experts in this area of juvenile crime view this as a Band-Aid approach to solve the problem. They stress the need to focus on support for these children, their families, and their communities rather than on punishment. "What's so disturbing," said Professor Felton Earls of the School of Public Health at Harvard University, "is to see a legal process that's lowering the age of adulthood rather than seeing this as a failure of social structures and policy towards our children."[2]

History. From colonial times until the late nineteenth century, children found guilty of crimes, even such as shoplifting, were jailed with violent criminals. No attention was given to their special needs. In 1899, in response to a society that was becoming more aware of, and concerned for, its younger members, a juvenile court was established in Chicago, and then soon throughout the nation. The prevailing belief was that the state would protect and guide the juvenile offenders by focusing on rehabilitation rather than on punishment. A "protective environment" was formed, but this proved to be a double-edged sword. Under the new system, juveniles were also denied the constitutional rights and protections afforded to adults under the Bill of Rights.

In juvenile court, judges had the twofold duty of balancing the interests of the child against the interests of society. Proceedings in a juvenile court were less formal than in an adult court. Private hearings were conducted without a lawyer or a jury. Judges considered oral and written reports made by probation officers, psychologists, and social workers regarding the background of the offender, the circumstances of the crime, and the gravity of the offense. Instead of jail, the offender was put on probation, or sent to a foster home, or reform school, or a state institution for juvenile delinquents. These actions, it was believed, would equip the child to re-enter society with little risk to the community.

Children, however, were still not protected by the rights guaranteed to all citizens by the Constitution. Although the reforms of juvenile court were initiated with the best interests of the child in mind, they also worked to the child's disadvantage. With no constitutional guidelines for protecting the child's procedural rights at the hearing, the fate of a child was left to the discretion of whichever judge was deciding the case. This arbitrary standard deprived the child of basic due-process rights (fair rules of procedure) that were standard for adults.

Turning Point in Children's Rights. It took what might be considered a relatively minor case to bring to center stage the issue of a child's constitutional rights when accused of a crime. Fifteen-year-old Gerald Gault of Arizona was arrested for making an obscene phone call to his neighbor, Mrs. Cook. He denied doing so, but was committed nevertheless to a state industrial school for six years by a judge of the juvenile court. (An adult would have been given a $50 fine or two months in jail.) This decision was made on the basis of a petition filed by a probation officer that stated that Gerald was a delinquent minor in need of protection by the juvenile court. His parents, however, were not served with a complaint. No sworn witnesses appeared at the hearing. Gerald continued to deny the accusation.

Despite the fact that appeals were not allowed in the Arizona juvenile court, Gerald's parents hired an attorney and challenged his sentence in federal court on the grounds that his constitutional rights were violated. In 1967, after Gerald had spent two years of his childhood in a state institution, the Supreme Court decided the case eight to one in his favor.

"Under our Constitution, the condition of being a boy does not justify a kangaroo court," said Justice Abe Fortas. The decision paved the way for future ones that would allow both the Fourteenth Amendment and the Bill of Rights to be applied to children, as well as adults. "We are to treat the child as an individual human being and not revert in spite of good intentions to the more primitive days when he was treated as chattel,"[3] continued Justice Fortas.

The rights of juveniles who find themselves in legal trouble were strengthened in 1974 when Congress passed the Juvenile Justice and Delinquency Prevention Act. This act stopped the automatic institutionalization of minors labeled as "status offenders," such as runaways and truants. It also ended the practice of jailing juveniles with adults, and it promoted the use of community-based rehabilitation programs for nonviolent offenders. Today, it is up to each state to determine the specifics of the juvenile justice system, such as age limits and sentences.

Rights of the Accused Minor. Since the case of Gerald Gault, minors are entitled to the due-process rights guaranteed under the Fourteenth Amendment. This means that they must be given advance notice of the charges against them, in order to have time to prepare for their defense. After the case of Dwight Lopez, this same right was extended to them in school: Students have a right to a hearing before they are suspended.

In 1975, Dwight Lopez, a high school senior, was suspended for ten days. His crime? A lunchroom fight that left school property damaged. Dwight challenged his suspension in court, stating not that he had not committed the crime, but that he had not been allowed a hearing, which, in legal terms, is the way an accused person can explain his or her actions in front of a judge. Dwight's case reached the Supreme Court.

The judges agreed that Dwight's suspension had violated his right to a hearing. They wrote in their opinion that Dwight had been deprived of his Fourteenth Amendment right to due process. In deciding the case, Supreme Court Justice Byron White wrote, "Young people do not shed their rights at the school room door."[4]

Minors are also protected by the Sixth Amendment, which gives them the right to have a lawyer represent them on a criminal charge. The Fifth Amendment gives them the right to remain silent, which protects against self-incrimination. Minors also have the right to confront witnesses who testify against them. However, children have no right to a jury in the juvenile court system. This is because the judge performs a more protective role in these proceedings than in adult court.

Arrest. A child can be taken into custody by a police officer if there is a "reasonable cause." Running away from home is reasonable cause, as is committing a delinquent act, or being suspected of a crime, or just being in a place considered dangerous to a minor's health and welfare. Attorneys advise minors if they are being detained or feel they are not free to walk away from the officer, whether it is on the street, in the police car, or in the precinct station, they should consider themselves under arrest.

And this is the point at which the precedent set in the Gault case starts working. Minors have the right to call a parent, guardian, or lawyer before answering any questions other than name, address, and telephone number. Threats, force, and coercion, on the part of an officer, are illegal. Miranda Rights—"You have the right to an attorney, and anything you say may be held against you in a court of law"—must be read to the minor by an officer of the law. An attorney must be present if the questioning is videotaped, and for the minor to participate in a police lineup.

The minor usually is released to his or her parent or guardian, unless the charge is a felony or there is need for protection. In that case the child may be put in a juvenile detention facility until the trial. A minor must be put in a center for juvenile offenders, if available— otherwise, in a separate division of an adult jail. Preventive detention is not punitive—that is, it should not deprive a child of proper treatment.

Unfortunately this fourteen-year-old boy is no stranger to the legal system. He was arrested and charged with carjacking, and it was not his first offense.

A minor may be brought to court pursuant to an arrest of a PINS (person in need of supervision) petition filed by a police officer, parent, or school official alleging that the minor's conduct is illegal or uncontrollable and that he or she is in need of supervision.

In the Courtroom. A "juvenile delinquent" is a minor, under the age of eighteen (in most states), who has broken the law and comes under the jurisdiction of juvenile court (sometimes called a family court). In some states, such as New York, the maximum age for juvenile court is sixteen. More serious felonies, such as murder, kidnapping, and arson, are waived into adult courts by a judge. (In some states this is determined by the prosecutor.) "Speedy trial" requirements ensure that the case is heard within a reasonable time period. The guidelines vary from state to state, but under the Federal Juvenile Delinquency Act the trial is usually held within thirty days. A juvenile is entitled to an attorney to help voice his or her own views especially if a "not guilty" plea is entered.

Juvenile courts also hear noncriminal actions involving PINS. They are minors who commit status offenses like running away from home or staying out of school. If a parent files a PINS petition with the court, a hearing is held to determine if the minor is in need of supervision. The minor has the right to have a lawyer present. If the judge declares a minor a PINS, he or she is usually put on probation and made to follow rules and report to a probation officer once a week or so. Minors who persist with the problem are usually sent to foster care or a group home until the judge rules that they are not in need of supervision or are too old to be in the category.

Not all complaints against juveniles reach a formal juvenile court hearing. It is estimated that almost 50 percent of complaints are decided at intake, a screening process conducted in an informal manner by a court official or a probation officer. This nonjudicial disposition, which is termed "diversion" in some states, results in the complaint being dismissed or referred to the supervision of a probation officer or a private community agency.

Court Dispositions. If the court finds that a juvenile is a delinquent, he or she is not automatically convicted of a crime. Generally, all court records are sealed and kept away from the public. After a dispositional hearing, where the juvenile is represented by a lawyer, the juvenile is either put on probation or sent to a juvenile detention facility or training school. The length of term and type of facility, which vary from state to state, are determined by the type of offense and background of the juvenile. In New York, the maximum sentence for someone under sixteen who commits group robbery in the second degree (the city's most common crime) is eighteen months. Usually only half of the sentence is served. The maximum sentence for an adult is fifteen years.

Politicians like Jeanne M. Adkins, chairwoman of the House Judiciary Committee, support legislation that, for certain crimes, would send juveniles to adult court. The belief is that the nature of the crime, not the age of the offender, should dictate the court and the sentence. "We've designed a system so lacking in accountability that those the system is designed to help mock it most."[5] Others feel it is the function of a judge to determine whether the child should be tried and convicted as an adult, based on a consideration of factors concerning not only society but also the specific child.

"The solution does not lie in mandated waivers, nor in most cases harsher sentences," says Circuit Court Judge David Mitchell. "Rather the solution lies in making changes in the juvenile system's approach to offenders. We need a series of graduated responses to juvenile crime, better community programs, and programs more responsive to changing times."[6]

Death Penalty. Capital punishment is allowed in thirty-five states. Over the past twenty years, seven of those executed were seventeen years old when they committed murder. The Supreme Court ruled in the case of *Thompson* v. *Oklahoma* (1988) that it is unconstitutional to execute someone who committed a crime at the age of fifteen, but one year later the Court ruled that someone who was sixteen at the time the crime was committed could be executed. Thompson, whose life was spared, said, "Prison has taught me all about respect for other people and patience."[7] During his trial, Thompson read on a fourth-grade level. Today, at twenty-three, he reads above the level of a high school senior and has earned his high school equivalency diploma.

The issue is whether juvenile murderers are recidivists (habitual criminals) who deserve to die or whether they should be given the opportunity to learn to live a more productive life.

Many juveniles on death row have psychiatric problems. Paula Cooper is an abused runaway from Indianapolis. Her parents were unmoved by the verdict of death against her. "They acted as if it was normal. They did not acknowledge that fact that I was sentenced to die." At fifteen she was sentenced to death for murdering a 78-year-old woman after a bout of drinking. Cooper's death sentence was set aside after the Thompson ruling. She will be eligible for parole when she is forty-five. "If I was still on the streets of Gary I'd probably be into all kinds of things: I could be a prostitute, a drug user, or I could be dead....One day I hope I can figure out how did I reach that point in my life where I got into that much trouble. A lot of kids like me must think about that, too."[8]

"It is a basic human notion that you don't hold juveniles to the same standard," said Victor Streib, a law professor and expert on juveniles on death row. "There are things we assume they are not responsible to do: drink, drive, get married. We all agree that at some age they can be treated as adults, but it is not a bright line. But killing kids in the name of justice is not something I want to support."[9]

Peer Pressure. Some approaches to fighting juvenile crime based on giving minors adult responsibilities along with their rights have also proven successful. One program "founded on the premise that young people who understand the nation's laws are less likely to violate them" allows first-time juvenile offenders to be sentenced by a jury of their peers.[10] Robert F. Stephens, chief justice of the Supreme Court of Kentucky and a promoter of this program, said: "Lack of knowledge, misinformation and confusion about the legal process lead to suspicion, disrespect and disregard of not only individuals who administer justice, but for the justice administered."[11]

The first teen court was started in Odessa, Texas, and since then, similar programs have followed in Arizona, Michigan, California, Florida, Indiana, and New

York. A case is first brought to a district court. If the judge recommends teen court, it is teens who will hear details of the case and deliver an appropriate and constructive sentence. "Sentencing is designed to hold youths accountable according to the idea that peer pressure exerts a powerful influence over adolescent behavior. If peer pressure leads juveniles into lawbreaking, it can be redirected to become a force in leading juveniles into law-abiding behavior."[12] Critics who say that teen courts are too lenient are refuted by the sentences handed down to guilty offenders. One minor, for example, charged with being intoxicated was given 105 hours of community service and a two-month curfew. The offender was also required to attend five Alcoholics Anonymous meetings and five sessions as a teen juror. And, unlike the overburdened social workers, teen court coordinators have the opportunity to monitor sentences given by the teen court. According to statistics, possibly 85 percent of the youths processed through teen courts will not end up as serious delinquents.

In New Haven, Connecticut, a truancy court targets middle-school students and young teenagers. In hopes that a court of their peers will not accept lame excuses, and will give to the young offenders the support needed to lure them back to school voluntarily, the Anti-Crime Youth Council, composed of students from area high schools and a law student from Yale University, gives the message that truancy is breaking the law. The consequence is juvenile court after twenty unexcused absences.

Parents Are Responsible. In an attempt to make parents assume some of the responsibility for their children's offenses, some states are punishing parents for the crimes committed by their children.

Eva Wilkinson of West Virginia served 100 days in jail because her daughter missed 59 days of school. In a Chicago suburb, parents receive a fine of $50 and 160 hours of community service if their children are caught skipping school, possessing liquor, or vandalizing. In Oregon, Anita Beck is challenging a similar ordinance after she was cited for her son's shoplifting. She is supported by the ACLU in her suit, which asserts that good parents can end up taking the blame for something they did not do.

According to the chief of police, juvenile crime has dropped in the first four months of this ordinance. "I don't think we're telling people how to parent," he said. "We're just giving them a tool to become better parents, trying to get at some of the parental apathy and neglect."[13] Michael Brock, whose father was cited for Michael's smoking, disagrees. "I'm still smoking cigarettes. They didn't do anything to me, but my dad got hauled into court and I don't think that's fair."[14]

Corporal Punishment. Corporal punishment is the infliction of physical pain or discomfort as a form of discipline. Public flogging was abolished in America in 1839, but more than half the states currently permit schools to use corporal punishment against their students. Laws that ban corporal punishment include provisions for teachers to use physical force to prevent immediate threats of harm to their person or property, or to get possession of weapons or dangerous objects.

In 1978, James Ingraham, a junior high school student in Florida, was sentenced to twenty licks with a paddle for walking too slowly off the stage of the school auditorium. His parents sued the school authorities. Paddling, said his lawyer, was a cruel and unusual punishment, which violated the Eighth Amendment. James's doctor would not let him return to school for eleven days. In a five-to-four decision, the Supreme Court ruled that it was not against the Constitution for the boy to have been paddled in instances where it is "reasonable and necessary" because the amount of supervision a community gives a school is safeguard enough against abuses. In other words, the community, not the Constitution, is the watchdog against cruel punishments in public schools.

In 1980 a federal appeals court in West Virginia found that a minor's constitutional rights were indeed violated by the use of excessive force against her by a teacher. The child spent ten days in the hospital after being paddled with a rubber paddle. The case did not reach the Supreme Court since the state of West Virginia did not appeal the decision. Research has found that corporal punishment is an ineffective method of controlling classroom behavior, yet more than a million schoolchildren are being hit by teachers, coaches, and principals each year.[15]

Sixteen-year-old Michael Fay became an instant celebrity when he was sentenced, in Singapore in 1994, to six painful and debilitating lashes with a wet rattan cane, for spray painting and vandalizing cars. Alleging that he confessed in order to stop the police from hitting him, he and his father were surprised that a large segment of the American population supported this punishment. The six lashes were reduced to four, when President Clinton interceded. In his home town of Kettering,

Michael Fay and his father smile as they leave
Singapore for the United States.

Ohio, Fay would have been fined, put on probation, and asked to pay damages to the owners of the cars.

Tribal Justice. Communities in the United States can mete out various types of punishment for criminal offenses. For instance, a landmark experiment in cross-cultural justice was attempted in Snohomish County, Washington. Adrian Guthrie and Simon Roberts, both seventeen and both members of the Tlingit Native American tribe, were found guilty of beating and robbing a pizza delivery man. Each boy was given a five-year sentence in a state prison, but the judge suspended this in favor of tribal justice. The Tlingit philosophy is to rehabilitate offenders by banishing them, giving them time to reflect alone on their life, and decide how best to cleanse it. In keeping with this, the tribal court banished the two boys to opposite ends of an uninhabited and remote island for twelve to eighteen months.

Although the concept of applying ancient American Indian philosophies of punishment and rehabilitation in state courts was appealing enough for the state judge to incorporate them into alternative sentencing structures, in practice it proved to be problematic. The legitimacy of the sentence was seriously compromised when it was discovered that relatives and members of the press had visited the island, and the boys were in constant contact with the mainland. The boys were returned to the mainland and were ordered by the court to complete their sentence in state custody.

Balancing Act. Balancing the rights of the accused and the rights of their victims is a problem that offers no easy solution. Whether beaten or mugged by a minor, or an adult, the victim has still been victimized. If society's responsibility, or ability, to protect itself is inconsistent with the rights of the individual, then whose rights should be primary? Some feel that the rights of the individual should be revoked, in the name of a peaceful society. "If we can't rehabilitate these kids, then let's at least isolate them," said Judge Judith Sheindlin of New York's family court.[16]

Others feel that punishment fails as a deterrent, especially with young people. These people believe that the crime is often committed as a rite of passage, and that increasing the sentence will make no difference. Minnesota Senator Patrick McGowan, who is also a detective sergeant, feels that although "people think you can change attitudes on violence overnight, you have to change whole generations of kids and the way they think. If you only have a treatment-prevention approach, the public is going to allow you time to change attitudes. You also have to hold criminals accountable. You have to stress both."[17]

A third group lies in between. According to UCLA Professor James Q. Wilson, a national expert on crime, penalties should take a first offense into consideration and increase in severity with each additional offense. In other words, don't wait for the big crime, but treat the child the way he or she is treated in the family—by dealing with each act as it happens.

Professor Steven Friedland, a juvenile-law expert, proposes the concept of "restorative justice," where justice would bring about healing. "Instead of viewing the acts of the offender as crimes against society, restorative justice uses mediation to allow victims to play a more central role in the criminal justice process. This substitute for incarceration or pure retribution promotes restitution and reconciliation." The offender is forced to "observe the human cost their actions have exacted."[18] In Oregon the Deschutes County Restorative Corps makes this concept a reality. Juvenile offenders perform work like clearing trees and building homeless shelters through public-service contracts, and victims receive their paycheck. According to the director of the program, "Kids leave the system more capable of making it in society than when they came in."[19]

City Challenge, a program in Brooklyn, New York, focuses on keeping juvenile offenders in school after their release from incarceration. Correction officials, criminologists, and educators are looking at regular schooling as a possible solution to prevent repeat offenders. The program allows offenders to complete their boot camp sentences in a school taught by public school teachers but supervised by the boot camp. City Challenge "tried to give youths the kind of individually tailored attention and supervision that experts have begun to consider crucial."[20]

Despite all the uproar about juvenile crime and punishment, there is some good news. Recent FBI records indicate that juvenile crime has been on the decline since 1993. The arrest rate for homicide for youths ages ten to seventeen has fallen 22.8 percent, while the overall rate for juvenile violent crimes, including assault, rape, robbery, and murder, has fallen 2.9 percent in one year. Janet Reno, the United States attorney general, attributes this decline to government policies, which included tougher sentencing laws, curfews, and prevention programs that support parents and communities in their efforts to supervise their children and keep them away from crime. Other experts credit the decline to better policing techniques practiced by law enforcement officials and the community. Although these statistics indicate a positive trend, Reno said that she shares this information with the American public "...to encourage communities to renew their efforts. We cannot relax. These rates are still far too high."[21]

CHAPTER NINE

A GLIMPSE INTO THE FUTURE

Whereas Mankind owes to the child the best it has to give.

UN Declaration of the
Rights of the Child, 1959

During the 1960s and 1970s America's youth emerged as an independent and forceful entity. Student protests on high school and college campuses demanded the attention of a nation. Their opinions on national policies were heard and addressed. Laws changed. Eighteen-year-olds, old enough to be sent to war, were finally declared old enough to vote, and the Supreme Court of the United States recognized that the Constitution of the United States also addressed the youth of America.

Caught up in the swell of this movement, one "child liberationist," John Holt, wrote in his book *Escape From Childhood* that children should be given all the rights and freedoms that adults have, to use at their discretion.

"If children do not learn the ropes faster in our society, and even now they learn them faster than we think, it is in part because they do not have to, are not expected to, and do not expect themselves to...in part because they know that they could not do anything with the knowledge if they had it."[1]

Richard Farson in his book *Birthright* recommended that children be given the right to vote because adults could not be trusted to vote in their best interests. First Lady Hillary Clinton, in an article for the *Harvard Educational Review*, challenged the validity of legally classifying every person under the age of eighteen or twenty-one as a minor. In effect, this deprived all "minors" of most enforceable adult rights. She pointed out that the "capacities and needs of a child of six months differ substantially from those of six or sixteen years."[2] She recommended a reevaluation of the "presumption of incompetence" of all minors and proposed that a child should be presumed competent until proven otherwise.

Although these thought-provoking ideas have influenced laws and attitudes concerning children, they are still viewed by many as extreme. Even though increased access to information through the media, as well as advancing technology, appears to accelerate the child's introduction into the adult world, the need for adult guidance and protection is still recognized by society and the law. The problem that society faces today in this complex environment is how to determine at which stage of development a child needs less protection and greater license to exercise freedom of choice. "What rights children should have ought to depend in part on what they need and want," says Laura Purdy in her book *In Their Best Interests:? The Case Against Equal Rights for Chil-*

dren. "But what they need and want depends in part on social conditions and social ideals."[3]

Children's rights are now undergoing something of a backlash. "A typical style is for the court to spend a few pages saying that the Bill of Rights applies to children and then to spend many more pages explaining why its OK to limit them,"[4] said Gary Melton, a children's law expert. The political and legal trend at the moment is toward restricting children's freedoms rather than expanding them. Many politicians point to the breakup of the family and juvenile crime as direct results of children having too much freedom, and parents too little control. The popular idea is to protect and preserve the child, and childhood, and delay adult responsibilities, unless the child is emancipated or commits an adult crime.

We have seen in this book that a delicate balance of power has to be maintained between the child, the parent, and the state. Children have some independent rights, parents have the rights and responsibilities concerning their children, and the state has an obligation to protect children. Recent shifts in the law have resulted in these three principles "colliding with each other." There is a definite threat that "if you push any of the three too far, it will erase the other two."[5]

The Gregory Kingsley case sent shock waves around the nation because it appeared that the rights of parents were taking a back seat to the rights of a child. In reality, the case strengthened the rights of the child to speak out when parents and the state do not fulfill their legal rights, responsibilities, and obligations. The larger threat to this balance of power occurs when laws are introduced by the state to not only limit the rights of children but also of parents. Curfew laws, work-restriction laws, and parent-liability laws are examples of this phenomenon. Parents are claiming that they are being stripped of their authority to set their own limits for their children and that they are being punished "simply for being a parent."[6] In response to these intrusions on parental autonomy, some federal lawmakers are planning to introduce a Parental Rights and Responsibilities Act, which would prevent federal, state, and local governments from "infringing on the right of parents to direct the upbringing and education of their children." Such legislation has not yet been passed at the state level. Colorado voted against a Parental Rights Amendment in the 1996 elections. On the federal level this proposed legislation is being challenged by several organizations, including the ACLU and the National PTA, for being overly broad and addressing "the rights of the parents without considering the needs of the children."[7]

Based on the philosophy that minors do not have the maturity to enjoy certain rights responsibly, the Supreme Court has limited these rights for children in a school-sponsored publication by giving the school officials the right to censor "inappropriate and unsuitable material."[8] Although a dissenting justice pointed out that this subjective standard for censorship was improper, the ruling still stands. Children, however, can still express themselves more openly in off-campus publications, enjoying the same First Amendment freedoms given to adults.

One solution to fighting the drug problem among youths has been for courts to curb the Fourth Amendment rights of minors. A lesser standard is applied to school officials who are agents of the state, when they are conducting searches for drugs or weapons, in the belief that this may deter violence and drug use among youths. The evidence discovered in these searches may be used to discipline the child and deprive him or her of freedom. However, if such evidence were discovered on an adult under similar conditions, it would be excluded from the trial because it would be violating the adult's Fourth Amendment rights.

Despite the rights secured in the case of Gerald Gault, children can still be deprived of their freedom for actions that would not be considered criminal among adults. These offenses include incorrigibility, truancy, and running away. In other words, for "the crime of having trouble growing up."[9]

The philosophy that a minor is immature, incapable, and in need of protection comes into question when the minor commits an adult crime. The state is then faced with the dilemma of whether to "protect minors from society or society from minors."[10] The juvenile justice system is criticized for being too sympathetic to the juvenile offender and out of touch with the times. For more than a hundred years after the system was created, minors have more rights and the line between childhood and adulthood is becoming less defined. However, "we are still dealing with a 1950s approach to juveniles back when it was a *Leave It to Beaver* kind of setting,"[11] says Florida Attorney General Bob Butterworth. Some politicians recommend a change of focus from rehabilitation to punishment of youthful offenders. While stiffer sentences may be necessary for violent offenders who are a real threat to society, many experts favor a less drastic approach for nonviolent offenders. Rather than responding to the crime and its impact on society in general, they favor a system that recognizes the level of competency of minors and the ability to force them to take responsibility for wrongful actions. Retribution is based on competency, and healing is the goal. Teen courts in Texas, tribal courts in Michigan, and Restorative Justice Corps in Oregon are testimonials to the success of these alternative approaches to combat juvenile crime.

Standing up for rights is not easy. It takes courage, commitment, and an understanding and appreciation of the responsibilities that accompany those rights. We have seen how kids like Claudette Colvin, Gregory Kingsley, the Tinker children, Ryan White, Benito Agrelo, and Desiray Bartak believed in the principle, participated in the legal process, and, with the support of their parents or guardians, fought for a right that is now enjoyed by others.

Organizations like the ACLU have also supported minors in their fights for constitutional rights, and they remain vigilant to challenge any actions that may violate these rights. The Children's Defense Fund, the United Nations, and Children's Rights, Inc., are organizations attuned to the special needs of the child. They continue in their commitment to preserve the child's independent legal rights. By providing legal support and advocating long-term solutions such as educational and social-welfare programs, they help to solve problems that affect the quality of a child's life. Perhaps an appreciation for those who sacrificed so much to fight for a hard-won right will inspire others to responsibly exercise the rights they have, and to work for other rights that are still needed. Whether the problem is as personal as Gregory's—fighting for a safe home—or as encompassing as the Tinkers' by protesting a war—every child has a right to be secure and safe and heard.

The future of children's rights lies in the hands of the state, the parents, and children themselves. As each era brings its own political, social, and economic challenges, there will be inevitable conflicts as each entity pursues its own standard of preserving the "best interests of the child." The difference between this century and its predecessors, however, is that children now have a real opportunity to voice their ideas on how to make the world a better, safer, and more equitable place for themselves. Perhaps if the voices of the children, parents, and the state act in unison to further this ideal, the rights of children may become synonymous with the needs of children.

Notes

Chapter One

1. James Kent, from lectures given from 1826–1830 in *Children and Youth in America*, Vol. 1, (Cambridge: Harvard University Press, 1970), p. 363.
2. In *Re Gault*, 387 US 1, 1967, on p. 87 (Volume 387 of the United States Reports Series beginning on page 1).
3. *Wisconsin v. Yoder*, 406 US 205 (1972).

Chapter Two

1. Joyce Purnik, "In a Vital Corner, Hearing the Call on Child Abuse," *New York Times*, Jan. 15, 1996, p. B1.
2. Debra West, "Shadowed by Suspicion," *New York Times*, October 19, 1995, p. B1.
3. Mark Sauer, "Create Family Preservation Programs" in the book *Child Abuse: Opposing Viewpoints*, Opposing Viewpoints Series, David Bender and Bruno Leone, Series Editors, (San Diego: Greenhaven Press Inc., 1994), p. 235.
4. Ibid., p. 238 (quoting Malcolm Bush from *Wounded Innocents* by Richard Wexler)
5. Ibid., p. 238.

6. Alan Finder, "The Pendulum of Policies on Child Abuse," *New York Times*, Jan. 12, 1996, p. B4.
7. Mary McGrory, "Defending Mommy Dearest," *Washington Post*, July 25, 1993, p. C1.
8. William Glaberson, "Child Custody Case Is Grist for High Court Test of Press Freedom," *New York Times*, Jan. 4, 1993, p. A10.
9. Raymond Hernandez, "Accord Eases Secrecy Rule on Abuse," *New York Times*, Feb. 1, 1996, p. A1.
10. Elizabeth Kastor, "The Girl Who Told Her Secret," *Washington Post*, Dec. 3, 1994, p. C1.
11. Ibid.

Chapter Three
1. Dirk Johnson, "Program Creates Community for Foster Care," *New York Times*, April 1, 1996, p. A1.
2. Pat Wingert and Elouise Salholz, "Irreconcilable Differences," *Newsweek*, September 21, 1992, pp. 84, 85.
3. Ibid., p. 85
4. Wiley B. Rutledge, *Prince v. Massachusetts*, 321 US 158, 166 (1944).
5. Pat Wingert and Elouise Salholz, "Irreconcilable Differences," p. 87.
6. Deborah L. Cohen, "Rights of Children, Roles of Families Eyed in Florida Case," *Education Week*, October 7, 1992, p. 21.
7. Anna Quindlen, "A Feeling Called Mama," *New York Times*, September 30,1992, p. A25.
8. Kenneth Jost, "Children's Legal Rights," *CQ Researcher*, April 23, 1993, p. 351, from "Families Divided: A Child's Day in Court," *Court TV*, January 10, 1993.
9. Anthony de Palma, "Custody Decision Dividing Experts," *New York Times*, September 27, 1992, p. 1:27.
10. Arnold Lubasch, "Boy in Divorce Suit Wins Right to Choose His Lawyer," *New York Times*, November 10, 1992, p. C3.
11. Arnold Lubasch, "11 Year Old in Custody Battle Wants to Trade in His Lawyer," *New York Times*, October 29, 1992, p. B6.
12. Deborah L. Cohen, "Rights of Children, Roles of Families Eyed in Florida Case," *Education Week*, October 7, 1992, p. 1.
13. *Dateline NBC*, January 17, 1996, transcript. National Broadcasting Company Inc.

14. "Custody of Deaf Girl Given to Sign Language Speaker," *New York Times*, June 3, 1995, p. 6.

15. Charles Sennott, "Torn Between Mothers," *Seventeen Magazine*, December 1993, pp. 114, 122.

16. Deborah L. Cohen, "Rights of Children, Roles of Families Eyed in Florida Case," *Education Week* (Quoting Leonard Loeb, a past president of the American Academy of Matrimonial Lawyers).

17. Joseph Goldstein, Anna Freud, and J. Albert Solnit, *Beyond the Best Interests of the Child*, (New York: The Free Press, 1973) p. 16.

18. David Gonzalez, "About New York— Seeking a Voice: The Children of Foster Care Write Their Own," *New York Times*, May 8, 1996, p. B1.

Chapter Four

1. Melanie J. Maurides, "Youth's Parody on the Internet Brings Punishment and a Free-Speech Fight," *New York Times*, May 28, 1995, p. 18.

2. Ibid.

3. Peter Lewis, "On-Line Services Join Indecency Lawsuit," *New York Times*, February 2, 1996, p. D2.

4. Ibid.

5. Doreen Rappaport, *Be the Judge, Be the Jury—Tinker v. Des Moines: Student Rights on Trial* (New York: HarperCollins, 1993), p. 142.

6. *Tinker v. Des Moines Independent School District*, 393 U.S. 503 (1966).

7. Ibid.

8. David A. Splitt, "When to Let Kids Express Themselves," *Executive Educator*, October 1994, p.17, reproduced in *SIRS Researcher* CD-ROM (Boca Raton, Fla.: SIRS, 1994)

9. *Hazelwood School District v. Kuhlmeier*, 484 U.S. 260 (1988). Justice William Brennan, Jr., dissenting.

10. Trip Gabriel, "The Ratings Game at the Cineplex," *New York Times*, February 18, 1996, p.1: 24-25.

11. Joel Friedman, "Rock & Roll Sharpens New Censor Scissor," *Billboard*, June 9, 1956, p. 18, reproduced in *SIRS Researcher* CD-ROM (Boca Raton, Fla.: SIRS)

12. *Board of Education, Island Trees Union Free School District No. 26 v. Pico*, 457 U.S. 853 (1982).

13. *Red Lion Broadcasting Co. v. FCC*, 395 U.S. 367 (1969).

14. "School Parents Call Halt to Use of Book on AIDS," *New York Times*, March 14, 1996, p. B7.
15. Jerry Gray, "School Prayer Debate Opens With Everything But Silence," *New York Times*, June 9, 1995, p. A20.
16. Ibid.
17. Ibid.
18. "Boots Make a Statement: Is It Fashion or Politics?" *New York Times*, November 5, 1993, p. A7.
19. Wayne King, "Curfew Vote in New Jersey Stirs Concern," *New York Times*, New Jersey Edition, September 18, 1882.
20. Ibid.
21. Robert Hanley, "Authorities Turn to Curfews to Clear the Streets of Teen-Agers," *New York Times*, November 8, 1993, p. B8.
22. Ibid. p. B1

Chapter Five
1. *Shields* v. *Gross* (Shields II) 186 NYLJ 4 (Sept. 29. 1981) (NY County Special Term) at 13.
2. *Shields* v. *Gross* (Shields I) A.D. 2d 846, 850, 451 N.Y.S. 2d. 419, 423 (1982) (quoting Brooke and Teri, January 19, 1982) at 65.
3. Shields II, 186 NYLJ at 13.
4. Charmaine Jefferson, "Mother Knows Best: Reconciling Parental Consent With Minor's Rights" in *Shields* v. *Gross Comm/Ent Hastings Journal of Communications* and *Entertainment Law*, Vol. 6, No. 3 Spring, 1984, p. 733.
5. Louis D. Brandeis, *Olmstead* v. *United States* 277 U.S. 438, 478 (1928) (dissenting).
6. Antonin Scalia, *Veronia School District* v. *Acton* No. 94-590 (1995).
7. Elinor J. Brecher and Sandra Jacobs, "A Drug Test Pits Parents' Concern v. Kids' Rights," *Miami Herald*, March 31, 1995, p. 1F, reproduced in *SIRS Researcher* CD-ROM (Boca Raton, Fla.: SIRS, 1995), *Privacy*, art. no. 115.
8. Ibid.
9. Ibid.
10. *Times* v. *Hill* 385 U.S. 374 (1967).
11. David Kidwell, "Girl Sues Show that Aired Rescue," *Miami Herald*, January 23, 1994, p. B1, reproduced in *SIRS Reasearcher* CD-ROM (Boca Raton, Fla.: SIRS, 1995), *Privacy*, art. no. 104.

12. Mark Twain, "License of the Press," (speech), Hartford, 1873, in *Writings of Mark Twain*, ed. Albert B. Paine (1929, pp. 28, 46, 46-47.

13. Ronald Fletcher, "Hearth and Home," *Society*, November/December 1993, p. 55 at p. 56.

14. Ibid., p. 60.

15. Newton N. Minow and Craig L. Lamay, *Abandoned in the Wasteland: Children, Television and the First Amendment* (New York: Hill & Wang, 1995), p. 138.

16. Ibid., p. 5.

17. Peter H. Lewis, "Judge Blocks Law Intended to Regulate On-Line Smut," *New York Times*, February 16, 1996, p. D1.

18. Gail B. Slap and Martha M. Jablow, "Debating Rights of Young Patients," *New York Times*, November 10, 1994, p. C1.

19. "Behind a Boy's Decision to Forego Treatment," *New York Times*, June 12, 1994, p. A7 (N) p. A12 (L).

20. Gail B. Slap and Martha Jablow, "Debating Rights of Young Patients," *New York Times*, November 10, 1994, p. C10.

21. Ibid., p. C10.

22. Holly Metz, "Branding Juveniles Against Their Will," *Student Lawyer*, February 1992, pp. 21, reproduced in *SIRS Researcher* CD-ROM (Boca Raton, Fla.: SIRS, 1992), *Youth*, Vol. no. 4, art. no. 23.

23. Christine Russell, "Abortion: Between Parent and Child," *Washington Post*, April 7, 1992, p. Health 11 and 13.

24. Ibid., p. 13.

25. Antonin Scalia, *Veronia School District* v. *Acton* No. 94-590 (1995).

26. David B. Rubin, "Passing Through the 'Schoolhouse Gate,'" Constitutional Implications of Preserving Student Safety," *Children's Legal Rights Journal*, Vol. 14, 1993, p. 21.

Chapter Six
1. Rosa Parks with Gregory J. Reid, *Quiet Strength* (Grand Rapids, MI: Zondervan Publishing House, 1994), p. 86.

2. Ellen Levine, *Freedom's Children* (New York: Avon Books, 1994), p. 27.

3. Richard Willing, "Civil Rights' Untold Story," *USA Today*, November 28, 1995, p. A1.

4. *Plessy* v. *Ferguson* 163 U.S. 537 (1896).
5. *Brown* v. *Board of Education* 347 U.S. 483 (1954).
6. Cynthia Durcanian and Ron Taylor, "Civil Rights: Is ERA Coming to an End?" *Atlanta Journal and Constitution*, July 2, 1989, p. A1, reproduced in *SIRS Researcher* CD-ROM (Boca Raton, Fla.: SIRS)
7. Stephen Labaton, "Denny's Restaurant to Pay $54 Million in Race Bias Suits," *New York Times*, May 25, 1995, p. A1.
8. Ronald Smothers, "Georgia Town Settles Suit Over Banning of Customers," *New York Times*, June 39, 1995 p. A10 (National), p. A12 (local).
9. Sara Rimer, "Challenge to Quotas Roils School in Boston," *New York Times*, September 25, 1995, p. A8.
10. Ibid.
11. Ibid.
12. Ibid.
13. Ibid.
14. "Elite Schools in Boston Plan End of Quotas," *New York Times*, Sunday, November 17, 1996, p. 30.
15. Ibid.
16. Stephen L. Carter, *Reflections of an Affirmative Action Baby*, (New York: HarperCollins, 1991), p. 7.
17. Elizabeth Levitan Spaid, "Faulkner's Battle Ends, But War Continues," *Christian Science Monitor*, August 21, 1995, p. 3.
18. Ronald Smothers, "Citadel Is Ordered to Admit a Woman to Its Cadet Corps," *New York Times*, July 23, 1994, p. A1.
19. Richard Lacayo, "To Hell Week and Back," *Time*, August 28, 1995, p. 36.
20. Sam and Beryl Epstein, *Kids in Court*. Four Winds Press, Division of Scholastic Inc., 1982, p. 178.
21. U.S. Department of Education Eighteenth Annual Report to Congress on the Implementation of IDEA, 1996.
22. Frank Bowe, *Equal Rights for Americans With Disabilities* (New York: Franklin Watts, 1992), p. 43.
23. Robert Horowitz and Adrienne Davis, "Pediatric AIDS, Emerging Policies," *Children's Legal Rights Journal,*, Vol. 7, No. 3, p. 5.
24. "Ryan White on His Life and His Fear," *Miami Herald*, April 1, 1990. (From transcript of the Phil Donahue Show aired November 25, 1988.) reproduced in *SIRS Researcher* CD-ROM (Boca Raton, Fla.: SIRS, 1990), AIDS, Vol.no. 2, art no.28.

Chapter Seven

1. James Warren, "White House Swings at Labor Law Curveball," *Chicago Tribune*, March 29, 1994, p. 12.
2. Author interview.
3. *The Chicago Tribune*, March 29, 1994, p. 12.
4. Sarah Norcliffe Cleghorn, "The Conning Tower," *New York Tribune*, June 1, 1915, found in *The Quotable Woman*, compiled by Elaine Partnow (Garden City, New York: Doubleday Anchor Books, 1978), p. 160.
5. Nancy Stancill, "Labor Law Enforcement Haphazard," *Houston Chronicle*, Jan.10, 1993, p. A10:2.
6. Nancy Stancill, "Underage Workers Frequent the Valley," *Houston Chronicle*, April 11, 1993, p. A1:1.
7. Stuart Silverstein, "Survey of Garment Industry Finds Rampant Labor Abuse," *Los Angeles Times*, April 15, 1994, p. D1:2.
8. In Brief, *Denver Post*, June 19, 1990, p. C1:2.
9. Author interview.
10. Ellen Graham, "Sprawling Bureaucracy Eats Up Most Profits of Girl Scout Cookies," *Wall Street Journal*, May 13, 1993, p. A1.
11. Author interview.
12. Lise Olson, "Labor Law Violators: Teens 'Want Extra Hours'," *Detroit News*, April 4, 1990, p. E1.
13. "Washington State Plans Tighter Child-Labor Rules," *New York Times*, August 17, 1992.
14. Ibid.
15. Daniel Sutherland and Martha M. Hamilton, "Food Lion to Settle Claims It Violated U.S. Labor Law," *Washington Post*, August 4, 1993, p. A3.
16. "Service With a Smile," *Seventeen Magazine*, January 1993, p. 24.

Chapter Eight

1. Fox Butterfield, "After a Decade Juvenile Crime Begins to Drop," *New York Times*, August 9, 1996, p. A1.
2. Alex Kotlowitz, "Their Crimes Don't Make Them Adults," *New York Times Magazine*, February 13, 1994, p. 41.
3. In Re Gault 387 US 1, 55 (1967).
4. *Goss v. Lopez* 419 US 565 (1975).
5. Jeanne M. Adkins and David B. Mitchell, "Is Adult Court the Place for Violent Teens?" *State Government News*, March, 1995,

pp. 36-37, reproduced in *SIRS Researcher* CD-ROM (Boca Raton, Fla.: SIRS, 1995), *Teen Courts*, Vol. no. 2, art. no. 83.

6. Ibid.
7. Kathryn Kahler, "Juvenile Murderers Face Death," *St. Paul Pioneer Press*, September 16, 1990, p. 1G, reproduced in *SIRS Researcher* CD-ROM (Boca Raton, Fla.: SIRS, 1990), *Corrections*, Vol. no. 4. art. no. 57.
8. Kathryn Kahler, "Murderer at 15, Saved From Execution at 19, Girl Now Looks to Future," *St. Paul Pioneer Press*, September 16, 1990, p. 4G, reproduced in *SIRS Researcher* CD-ROM (Boca Raton, Fla.: SIRS, 1990), *Corrections*, Vol. no. 4. art. no. 57.
9. Ibid.
10. Deborah Williamson and others, "Teen Court—Juvenile Justice for the 2First Century?" *Federal Probation*, Administrative Office of the Third U.S. Courts, pp. 54-58, reproduced in *SIRS Researcher* CD-ROM (Boca Raton, Fla.: SIRS, 1993), *Corrections*, Vol. no. 5, art. no. 12.
11. Ibid.
12. Ibid.
13. Timothy Egan, "When Young Break Law, A Town Charges Parents," *New York Times*, May 31, 1995, p. A1.
14. Ibid.
15. Cindy S. Moelis, "Banning Corporal Punishment: A Crucial Step Towards Preventing Child Abuse," *Children's Legal Rights Journal*, Vol. 9, No. 3, U.S. Department of Education (Information from Office of Civil Rights, (1986-87).
16. Craig Horowitz, "Law and Disorder," *New York Magazine*, January 10, 1994, p. 25.
17. Penelope Lemov, "The Assault on Juvenile Justice," *Governing*, December 1994, pp. 26-31, reproduced in *SIRS Researcher* CD-ROM (Boca Raton, Fla.: SIRS, 1994), *Youth*, Vol. no. 4, art. no. 80.
18. Steven Friedland, "The Rhetoric of Juvenile Rights," *Stanford Law and Policy Review*, Vol. 6, No. 2, 1995, p. 137 at 144.
19. Ibid.
20. Pam Belluck, "The Youngest Ex Cons: Facing a Difficult Road Out of Crime," *New York Times*, November 17, 1996, pp. 1 and 40.
21. Fox Butterfield, "After 10 Years Juvenile Crime Begins to Drop," *New York Times*, August 9, 1996, p. A1.

Chapter Nine

1. John Holt, *Escape From Childhood* (New York: E.P. Dutton, 1974), p. 97.
2. Hillary Rodham, "Children Under the Law," *Harvard Educational Review*, Vol. 43, No. 4, November 1973, p. 489.
3. Laura Purdy, *In Their Best Interests: The Case Against Equal Rights for Children* (Ithaca, New York: Cornell University Press, 1992), p. 12.
4. Kenneth Jost, "Children's Legal Rights," *CQ Researcher*, April 23, 1993, p. 340.
5. Ibid. (Quoting Robert Mnookin, p. 340).
6. Timothy Egan, "When Young Break Law, A Town Charges Parents," *New York Times*, May 31, 1995, p. A1.
7. Peter Applebome, "An Array of Opponents Do Battle Over 'Parental Rights' Legislation," *New York Times*, May 1, 1996, p. A1, B7. (Quoting Shirley Igo, vice president for legislation with the National PTA).
8. *Hazelwood School District* v. *Kuhlmeier* 484 US 260 (1988).
9. Hillary Rodham, *Harvard Educational Review*, 1973, p. 491.
10. Steven Friedland, "The Rhetoric of Juvenile Rights," *Stanford Law and Policy Review*, Vol. 6, No. 2, 1995, p. 137 at p. 140.
11. Mike Clary, "Execution of Teen-Age Killers Weighed," *Los Angeles Times*, October 8, 1993, p. A20.

Selected Bibliography
For Further Reading

Alderman, Ellen and Caroline Kennedy. *The Right to Privacy*. New York: Alfred A. Knopf, 1995.

Bender, David and Bruno Leone, Editors. *Child Abuse: Opposing Viewpoints*. San Diego: Greenhaven Press Inc., 1994.

Bowe, Frank. *Equal Rights for Americans With Disabilities*. New York: Franklin Watts, 1992.

Carter, Stephen L. *Reflections of an Affirmative Action Baby*. New York: HarperCollins, 1991.

Cunningham, AnnMarie. *Ryan White, My Own Story*. New York: Dial Books, 1991.

Fuson, Harold W., Jr. *Telling It All: A Legal Guide to the Exercise of Free Speech*. Kansas City: Andrews & McMeel, 1994.

Guggenheim, Martin and Alan Sussman. *The Rights of Young People*. New York: Bantam Books, 1985.

Kittredge, Mary. *Teens With AIDS Speak Out*. New York: Julian Messner, 1991.

Landau, Elaine. *Your Legal Rights*. New York: Walker & Co., 1995.

Minow, Newton and Craig Lamay. *Abandoned in the Wasteland: Children, Television, and the First Amendment.* New York: Hill and Wang, 1995.

Newton, David. *AIDS Issues: A Handbook.* New Jersey: Enslow Publishers, 1992.

Purdy, Laura. *In Their Best Interests? The Case Against Equal Rights for Children.* Ithaca, NY: Cornell University Press, 1992.

Amendment I [1791]

Congress shall make no law respecting an establishment of religion, or prohibiting the free exercise thereof; or abridging the freedom of speech, or of the press; or the right of the people peaceably to assemble, and to petition the Government for a redress of grievances.

Amendment II [1791]

A well regulated Militia, being necessary to the security of a free State, the right of the people to keep and bear Arms, shall not be infringed.

Amendment III [1791]

No Soldier shall, in time of peace be quartered in any house, without the consent of the Owner, nor in time of war, but in a manner to be prescribed by law.

Amendment IV [1791]

The right of the people to be secure in their persons, houses, papers, and effects, against unreasonable searches and seizures, shall not be violated, and no Warrants shall issue, but upon probable cause, support by Oath or affirmation, and particularly describing the place to be searched, and the persons or things to be seized.

Amendment V [1791]

No person shall be held to answer for a capital, or otherwise infamous crime, unless on a presentment or indictment of a Grand Jury, except in cases arising in the land or naval forces, or in the Militia, when in actual service in time of War or public danger; nor shall any person be subject for the same offence to be twice put in jeopardy of life or limb; nor shall be compelled in any criminal case to be a witness against himself, nor be deprived of life, liberty, or property, without due process of law; nor shall private property be taken for public use, without just compensation.

Amendment VI [1791]

In all criminal prosecutions, the accused shall enjoy the right to a speedy and public trial, by an impartial jury of the State and district wherein the crime shall have been committed, which district shall have been previously ascertained by law, and to be informed of the nature and cause of the accusation; to be confronted with the witnesses against him; to have compulsory process for obtaining witnesses in his favor, and to have the Assistance of Counsel for his defence.

Amendment VII [1791]

In Suits at common law, where the value in controversy shall exceed twenty dollars, the right of trial by jury shall be preserved, and no fact tried by jury, shall be otherwise re-examined in any Court of the United States, than according to the rules of the common law.

Amendment VIII [1791]

Excessive bail shall not be required, nor excessive fines imposed, nor cruel and unusual punishments inflicted.

Amendment IX [1791]

The enumeration in the Constitution, of certain rights, shall not be construed to deny or disparage others retained by the people.

Amendment X [1791]

The powers not delegated to the United States by the Constitution, nor prohibited by it to the States, are reserved to the States respectively, or to the people.

LATER AMENDMENTS

Amendment XIII [1865]

Section 1. Neither slavery nor involuntary servitude, except as a punishment for crime whereof the party shall have been duly convicted, shall exist within the United States, or any place subject to their jurisdiction.

Section 2. Congress shall have power to enforce this article by appropriate legislation.

Amendment XIV [1868]

Section 1. All persons born or naturalized in the United States, and subject to the jurisdiction thereof, are citizens of the United States and of the State wherein they reside. No State shall make or enforce any law which shall abridge the privileges or immunities of citizens of the United States nor shall any State deprive any person of life, liberty, or property, without due process of law; nor deny to any person within its jurisdiction the equal protection of the laws.

Section 2. Representatives shall be apportioned among the several States according to their respective numbers, counting the whole number of persons in each State, excluding Indians not taxed. But when the right to vote at any election for the choice of electors for President and Vice President of the United States, Representatives in Congress, the Executive and Judicial officers of a State, or the members of the Legislature thereof, is denied to any of the male inhabitants of such State, being twenty-one years of age, and citizens of the United States, or in any way abridged, except for participation in rebellion, or other crime, the basis of representation therein shall be reduced in the proportion which the number of such male citizens shall bear to the whole number of male citizens twenty-one years of age in such State.

Section 3. No person shall be a Senator or Representative in Congress, or elector of President and Vice President, or hold any office, civil or military, under the United States, or under any State, who, having previously taken an oath, as a member of Congress, or as an officer of the United States, or as a member of any State legislature, or as an executive or judicial officer of any State, to support the Constitution of the United States, shall have engaged in insurrection or rebellion against the same, or given aid or comfort to the enemies thereof. But Congress may by a vote of two-thirds of each House, remove such disability.

Section 4. The validity of the public debt of the United States, authorized by law, including debts incurred for payment of pensions and bounties for services in suppressing insurrection or rebellion, shall not be questioned. But neither the United States nor any State shall assume or pay any debt or obligation incurred in aid of insurrection or rebellion against the United States, or any claim for the loss or emancipation of any slave; but all such debts, obligations and claims shall be held illegal and void.

Section 5. The Congress shall have power to enforce, by appropriate legislation, the provisions of this article.

Amendment XV [1870]

Section 1. The right of citizens of the United States to vote shall not be denied or abridged by the United States or by any State on account of race, color, or previous condition of servitude.

Section 2. The Congress shall have power to enforce this article by appropriate legislation.

Index